COMMUNITY Policing:

The Path to Healthier Relationships

...a Police Chaplain's Perspective

Dr. Francis (Munangi) Mpindu, PhD

Community Policing

Copyright © 2020 by Dr. Francis (Munangi) Mpindu, PhD

Tellwell Talent
www.tellwell.ca

ISBN
978-0-2288-3362-8 (Hardcover)
978-1-9992787-0-0 (Paperback)

Table of Contents

Chapters

This book is dedicated to...

The Community. You continue to contribute to and influence my identity and my deep sense of belonging to the human race (*Ubuntu*) in remarkable ways. I am who I am because of who we all are.

The Police Officers. You are community engagers and practitioners. Out of your own volition and commitment to serve people and make our communities safe, you have answered the call to join one of the noblest careers in the world. You serve and protect our communities each day—24/7, 365 days of the year. You have obtained rigorous specialized training that equipped you to be incessant conflict resolution practitioners. You willingly put your lives on the line as you serve and protect lives and property. You ensure that the laws of the land and the charter of rights and freedoms are upheld within the context of social justice, human rights, and professionalism so that we can live amicably in our inter-culturally diverse communities.

My Mother, Susan Shupikai Mpindu. From a young age, you taught me by example the value of building and maintaining healthy relationships with people. One of those significant lessons was that 'Some people may choose to dislike you and even choose to mistreat you, but they cannot choose how you should treat them in return.' Indeed, I am responsible for my attitude and actions toward other people.

No one causes me to say or do something hurtful to another human being. I can choose to say or do the right thing in any situation.

My Daughters, Tariro (Linda), Rutendo (Mildred), and *Niece* Nyasha (Martha). Life is so daily. As you rub shoulders with others each day, I pray that you continue to develop your conflict management skills and establish healthier relationships in life. Remember, unresolved disputes and conflicts are very costly.

Preface

This book covers a timely topic.

We live in a time of great uncertainty when people increasingly engage in quests for answers, information, guidance, support, and protection in all dimensions of life. That is where the police and the community need to work collaboratively to provide solutions. When tensions run high between them, both parties need to Dialogue, Discover, and Decide – on the best way forward. They need to trust and respect each other by sustaining the existing bridges of collaboration and building new ones. This book appeals to our desperately needed collective sense of civility. It invites the community and the police into the PATH to healthier relationships as we journey together. Indeed, we need each other. After all, we are on the same team.

Generally, a book idea is triggered by something. It is a response, an attempt to provide a solution to some issue or problem, some challenge, or some dissatisfaction. This book is no exception.

The inspiration to write this book emerged from a combination of at least five sources:

1. I often thought about the value of putting a resource in the hands of each new immigrant to help them learn about policing in Canada. In York Region, the police works with the Ministry of Immigration, Refugees and Citizenship, a judge who administers the oath, and numerous local representatives and community partners to organize and celebrate the welcoming of new Canadian.

2. My insights from conversations with friends and individuals (residents and citizens) in various culturally

diverse backgrounds about their perspectives, perceptions, and experiences with the police here and other police jurisdictions in different countries;

3. Insights from reading "Enhancing York Regional Police's Relationship with its Visible Minority Communities" by Police Chief Eric Jolliffe for his Master of Arts thesis in Leadership at Royal Roads University, 2012;

4. Insights from taking the postgraduate Certificate in Alternative Dispute and Conflict Resolution at York University; and

5. Insights from my ongoing services and participation as a police chaplain over the past sixteen years. This context has given me countless opportunities to observe both the community and the police in real time.

This book is written from various perspectives that reflect who I am in relation to others. I am writing as a member of the community who happens to be an alternative dispute and conflict resolution, negotiation and mediation practitioner, a family member, a father, a Zimbabwean-born Canadian (ZBC), a religious/spiritual leader, a police chaplain, an academic, and as an African Canadian. These various contexts and social connections colour my perspectives in subtle and overt ways and influence how I tell my story in this book. I write all of this, while seeking to avoid the "danger of a single story"[1] as beautifully articulated by Chimamanda, a Nigerian storyteller.

This book has a dual purpose. First, I hope to assist fellow Canadians (newer and older immigrants, and those born in Canada) to consciously and subconsciously engage in a learning process of adjusting their mindsets, perspectives, and worldviews about the police and policing in Canada, and embrace a culture of relating to them constructively.

---

[1] See TED Talks: The danger of a single story, Chimamanda Ngozi Adichie. (TEDGlobal) October 2009. In this presentation, Chimamanda scores good points on inviting all of us to allow other people's stories to influence our own storytelling so that we share stories that are complete and more inclusive.

Second, I hope to assist police officers to engage intentionally in "learning conversations"[2] and strategic relational dynamics in community engagement as skilled alternative dispute and conflict resolution and mediation professionals. Indeed, there is wisdom in the police being intentionally curious, proactive, and humble enough to engage in ongoing learning and developing healthy interactive conversations with the people in the community. It is through these intentional community engagements that the police may be perceived and accepted as resources and professionals who care enough to partner with the people and police our communities effectively as community engagers, alternative dispute and conflict resolution, negotiation, and mediation practitioners.

The book's dual purpose makes it a difficult and special treatise, and one that aims at bringing the two partners—community and the police—into an intentionally healthy working relationship. Thus, favouring one partner over the other has the potential of losing the other, and thus deviating from the objective of the book. You, the reader, will be the judge.

This book contains ten chapters. Chapter 1 brings a perspective on experiences with the police overseas and shows how those experiences can colour one's present perspectives and interactions with the police in Canada and around the globe. Chapter 2 provides a synopsis of my journey to Canada, starting with my first exposure to life here during my elementary school geography class as a little boy in Zimbabwe. Chapter 3 explains how I became a police chaplain, and Chapter 4 describes what police chaplains do (or are supposed to do), showing that there are at least two categories of chaplains. Chapter 5 highlights the fundamental philosophies or theoretical principles that are designed to guide how the police operate in Canada; that is, the notion of "policing with the community" and not "policing the community." Chapter 6 presents the four key engagements of frontline policing, and Chapter 7 discusses some of the most challenging realities faced by frontline police officers in the course of carrying out their duties and responsibilities within culturally diverse

[2] Douglas Stone, Bruce Patton, Sheila Heen. Difficult Conversations: How to Discuss What Matters Most. Penguin Books, 1999. All three authors are distinguished lecturers at Harvard University.

contexts. Chapter 8 shares a religious and cultural perspective. As human beings, whether we are people of faith or people of no faith or organized religion, we all subscribe to some deity or force/power that influences our belief systems and behaviour. Chapter 9 offers practical suggestions on how the police and the community may break down the socio-cultural barriers that impede the creation, cultivation, or leveraging of trust-based environments that lead to the path of healthier relationships. Finally, Chapter 10 concludes this discussion and provides some takeaways. There is a two-part appendix covering (a) an abbreviated biography of the author and (b) some community resources recommended by the author.

As immigrants to Canada, we come from many different countries and bring with us variable information, life experiences, expectations, observations, interpretations, and conclusions about the police. There is great value and wisdom in learning about the police and how policing is done in our chosen country of residence.

It can be challenging for members of the community and the police alike to get along due to past experiences. Information has been obtained, observations gained, perceptions developed, and interpretations created about each other. The task of shifting perceptions, cognitive processes, and behaviours is complex. We all bring our *katundu* ((Shona word for baggage) from the past, which inexorably colours our present interactions. To have healthier relationships between the community and the police, both sides need to place high value on the relationship itself, then commit to identifying intentional steps toward connecting and building that relationship for mutual benefit.

The idea of intentionally seeking to build healthier relationships between the community and the police was new territory for me. The journey began a little over twenty-nine years ago, after I came to Canada. This is a nation made up of immigrants—newer or older immigrants, or children of immigrant parents—except for our indigenous friends, the First Nations, the Inuit, and the Métis (FNIM). Sadly, sometimes 'older immigrants' with selective memory blurt out negative comments about newer immigrants coming to "our country to enjoy Canadian benefits, and change things in their favour." Aside from the First Nations, Inuit, or Métis, a gentle and firm reminder may be warranted. Say to them, "Remember, we are all immigrants here, except for the indigenous people. It might have taken me a little longer to come to Canada than you and your family did, but I got here as quickly as I could, and I am a full Canadian as you are. Let us learn to enjoy our culturally diverse nation."

One of the realities in our major urban cities across Canada today is that the so-called "visible minorities" born outside of Canada have now become the visible majority. Back in 2011, Statistics Canada reported that, of the 6.2 million people who identify themselves as members of visible minority groups, 65.1% of that population were born outside Canada. The three largest visible minority groups were South Asians, Chinese, and Blacks. These three groups accounted for 61.3% of the population of Canada in 2011. This information tells a big story about the Canadian "cultural mosaic," a term introduced by John Murray Gibbon way back in 1938.[3]

I am both a proud Zimbabwean and a proud Canadian. I am a "ZBC"—a Zimbabwean-born Canadian—according to my compatriot, friend, and older brother, Dr. Roy Musasiwa. He is the principal of Domboshawa Theological College in Harare, and I think this is an insightful and fitting label of who I am.

This book reflects conversations with my two daughters (Linda, *Tariro* and Mildred, *Rutendo*) and niece Martha *Nyasha* – when they were younger, after I became a chaplain with York Regional Police. Upon seeing a police officer or a police cruiser, they would remark, "Hey Dad, there is your friend." They made this remark quite often, and I would respond affirmatively. I did my best to turn that into a teaching moment about our relationship with the police. As time progressed, I would say, "I surely hope that one day you girls will be able to say, 'Hey Dad, look, there are *our* friends.'" They responded with big beautiful smiles. Thank you girls for your input into this book project! You got

---

[3] John Murray Gibbon argued against the American idea of a "cultural melting pot" that encouraged immigrants to cut ties with their culture of origin and assimilate into a homogenous society. This is now part of the Canada Multiculturalism Act of 1988, which reflects the changing reality of racial and ethnic diversity policy. It emphasizes the right of all individuals to preserve and share their cultural heritage while retaining their right to full and equitable participation in Canadian society... https:www.theCanadianEncyclopedia-ca/en/article/john-murray-gibbon-emc.1938.

me on the path to provide a tool to help many people to build better relationships with the police.

This book aims to facilitate healthier relationships between the community and the police. I am aware that this is a complex task, but the rewards are priceless.

I hasten to mention that this book expresses my personal views, influences of and from other people (directly and/or indirectly), observations and interpretations of other people's works informed by my limited knowledge, subjective assumptions, and my own biases. Indeed, I take full responsibility for any errors, misrepresentations, and shortcomings.

Chapter One
Life on the Other Side of the Atlantic Ocean

I was born at Harare Central Hospital in Zimbabwe. I am the first of three boys: Francis, Amos, and Takesure, who died as an infant. My parents bumped into each other in the capital city, Harare, back in their early days, and grew to like each other. My father, Mr. Sonny Munangi, worked at the famous Northwest Bakery in the Mabelreign Shopping Centre. They used to make some of the yummiest eats on planet earth. My mother, Miss Susan Mpindu, worked in the city for a white family as a maid. Not long after my brother and I were born, Mom was strongly encouraged (basically told) to move out of the city and be a housewife in rural Zaka, Masvingo, away from her familiar environment. This was a drastic change for a city girl, who needed lots of support and different sets of life skills to adjust to a new context. By the time I was three years old, my parents' common-law relationship had deteriorated so much that they went their separate ways. Mom moved with us (the two boys) back to the city. The journey was tough on her. She told us of how she packed all her stuff and our clothing into plastic bags to board the bus, and how some Good Samaritans shared their food with us when we got hungry. Needless to say, it was difficult for our mother to raise two boys as a single parent.

Since our father was not with us anymore, Mom worked hard as a maid for several white families to provide us with a foundation for formal education. Apparently, when my brother and I were born, our father had not provided his national registration card to enable us to obtain birth certificates under his surname, Munangi. Instead, our uncles from the Mpindu side of the family ensured that we obtained birth certificates using their legal documents in preparation to attend school. It was our late great-grandpa (*sekuru*) Elijah Mpindu, who made sure that our uncles accepted us as "Mpindu children," even though we were not necessarily treated that way, sometimes. When we finally started school, it dawned on us that there was a stigma attached to not having your father's last name, especially when other kids in the school discovered the truth about our family situation. Even our uncles made it abundantly clear to everyone in the community that we were not their real children, and that our father was "somewhere out there." On the other hand, Grandma Evangelista (vaMudadi) was a breath of fresh air. She had a heart of gold, always made us feel special, and showered us with expressions of love, care, and words of affirmation.

However, one uncle from my father's side of the family, the late Winston Sungano Munangi, stayed in touch with Mom and us over those years. He facilitated my first meeting with my father the year I turned twenty. Uncle Winston, affectionately called Daddy Winston, and his wife, Auntie Esther, occupy a special place in our family tree. Growing up in the Zimbabwe Shona culture, it was regarded as a sign of disrespect to refer to them as *aunt* and *uncle* because that would imply that they were distant relatives. Such categorizations would be an insult to them and my close family members.

Therefore, in honour of, and in appreciation for, these two special families in my life, who have contributed remarkably to who I am, I use both surnames, with Munangi in brackets since that is not included on my legal documents.

Although our mother had numerous limitations and strikes against her, such as coming from a poor family, having only elementary school education, and walking with a pronounced limp because she had suffered polio as a little girl, she believed that she could rise up against the odds. She had such a high value for education, and so she went out of her way to learn to speak and write in English and attain a good command of the language—enough to articulate it with clarity, confidence, and market herself in different contexts. Furthermore, she developed a high value for investing in and providing us (her sons) with a solid foundation for formal education. She would constantly buy us books to read. That contributed early in my life to a strong love and fascination with books. Even as a high school student, I would carry around a novel to read because Mom had instilled in me the importance of reading books to broaden my knowledge.

I recall that we had a compact radio and record player system that also preoccupied us. Mom liked country western music like Dolly Parton, Kenny Rogers, and Don Williams. Every now and then, we found ourselves playing music, listening to news, and hearing a famous children's educational and national "greetings" program by Mbuya Chirambakusakara.

No wonder my mother became my number one fan, cheering me on as I finished primary school, high school, and went on to attend various colleges in Zimbabwe, Kenya, Canada, and South Africa. When I was completing my PhD program from the University of Pretoria (South Africa), there was one person I did not want to miss my graduation in April 2003. I wanted her to watch me being capped, to ululate, hug me, and congratulate me, and to say "Well done. Yes, we did it." That was my mother, Susan Shupikai Mpindu. Mom ended up missing my graduation because she died on January 19, 2003, after a short illness. That was one of the most difficult days in my life, graduating without my #1 fan. However, my mother, being a good planner, had 'made arrangements' to have someone take her place. This beautiful middle-aged black South African woman, within her age bracket, walked up to me at the end of the graduation ceremony and said, "Congratulations, son. I am sure your mother is proud of you." On hearing those words, I was overwhelmed with emotions. My eyes welled up with tears, I pulled out my handkerchief from my back pocket, and by the time I put myself together, she was gone. I recall this experience vividly and cherish it every time I reflect on that graduation. Indeed, South Africa and Zimbabwe have contributed in large ways to who I am today. I must also add Kenya, Jamaica, and Canada to that list.

Zimbabwe, formerly Rhodesia, is a relatively young nation established on April 18, 1980. Prior to that time, racism, segregation, and racial inequity (discrimination) were the order of the day. Growing up, there were (and still are) four distinct groups of people: blacks, whites, coloureds, and Indians (East Indians). Black Africans (the Shona and the Ndebele people) are the natives of Zimbabwe from time immemorial. Whites came to Zimbabwe shortly after Cecil John Rhodes' arrival from Great Britain in 1890. As the white population increased and settled, some of the white men were pleasantly surprised to discover how beautiful black women were, and consequently, the

Coloured race started. The Indians began settling in Zimbabwe from South Africa as early as the 1890s also.

As a little boy, my world was challenging. All the residential areas in the towns and cities, all the schools, hospitals, places of worship, shops, and the public transport system across the country were segregated, reflecting the racial fragmentation with all the related social pathologies. Even at the national university, the University of Rhodesia (now University of Zimbabwe), the racist regime intentionally determined how many black people would be enrolled each year, and influenced what faculties they would get into. In the final analysis, the workforce structure and composition were pre-determined by a minority group.

In Salisbury, the capital city (now Harare), black people were not allowed to be on certain streets, especially in the city centre, unless they had a permission note. They were required to carry permission cards (special IDs) or notes to justify their presence in that part of the city in their native country. Furthermore, the blacks were prohibited from using the only underground washrooms (toilets/restrooms) in the city centre, on First Street. The toilets had big signs at the entrance that read, "For Whites Only." Indeed, these were painful expressions of inequality and inequity embedded in the political and socio-economic system in all dimensions of life across the nation.

Police officers (or as we referred to them – policemen and policewomen) were neither liked nor respected. We referred to them by two distinct categories: *mapurisa/amapolisa,* "black police officers," and *majoni/amajoni* (Shona and Ndebele words), "white police officers." There was a clear distinction between black and white to warrant such categories even within the police. In fact, like most people in Zimbabwe, I grew up in an environment with overt hatred and distrust for the police. For example, I "knew" that:

- the police was a symbol of an oppressive and racist government

- the police could slap you, beat you up, kick you, and arrest you anytime they thought you deserved it

- the police disliked blacks and favoured whites and coloureds

- only blacks were arrested and sent to jail by the police

- the black police officers were the white man's puppets, and

- black police officers were always low-ranked and were not promotable to senior ranks.

The Rhodesia Police wore brass lapels on their shoulders with the initials BSAP, for British South Africa Police. To the black Shona folks, the acronym BSAP meant "*Bhururu, Satani Ari Pano,*" which translates to "Friend, Satan is here." The police officers were viewed and recognized as the epitome of evil. They did not have a good reputation among black people, and so they were disliked by the greater population.

However, there were some exceptions. One such rare breed of police officer, highly respected and appreciated in the community, was Member in-Charge Thomas Choto, who headed the Police Station in Glen Norah A — a high-density suburb of Harare. Officer Choto was a senior officer who valued connecting with people and establishing healthy friendships in his neighbourhood. Somehow, he had figured out how to balance policing and hanging out with people (engaging the community) without compromising his position and duties as an officer. His friendly disposition made it easy for people to approach him and share their police-related matters with him, knowing that he would provide the needed information or resolve the issues. Choto accorded remarkable respect in the Glen Norah area and beyond. Indeed, he had earned the trust of the people as a friend and a professional in the community. We were always intrigued by his ability to arrest law breakers and criminals in the neighbourhood, maintain approachability, and engage in crime prevention, yet continue to be respected as a friend and a professional in the community.

There were other problems, though. If a child was crying and the parents failed to stop the child by means of negotiation, they commonly threatened to hand the child over to the police for a good spanking or some jail time. Unhealthy fear of the police was introduced at such an early age. If police officers were patrolling the streets on foot, horsebacks, bicycles, or in their cars, people did all they could to avoid contact with them. People often ran away from officers in uniform, despite not having done anything wrong or illegal. We simply stayed as far away from the police as we could and sought to maintain a safe distance. An unhealthy fear of the police continued.

If the police stopped you on the street, you always expected the worst treatment. Zimbabwe's police had a bad reputation of terrorizing people for no apparent reason, it seemed. They could beat you up, slap you, kick you, handcuff you, threaten you, or lock you up in the cell with no regard for accountability to anyone. They could do anything to people and get away with it. The police was likened to an organized (and legalized) gang that terrorized people whenever they saw fit.

If the police came to your door, your neighbours would look upon you with suspicion. Such a visit carried the social stigma that you were trouble with a capital T. Neighbours would wonder whether you were a criminal or an informant. In either case, police at your house signalled your 'bad character' in the neighbourhood. You could not be trusted anymore.

People generally connected with the police only when they wanted police services. Basically, the relationship would be described as, "I will call on you when I need your assistance; you should help me by invitation only or when I am in need; otherwise, I desire no association with the police at all other times. Please stay away from me." Consequently, few parents openly encouraged their children to consider policing as a noble career path. If a member of the family were to become a police officer, the family would be shunned and labelled as sell-outs—people who betrayed their community by aligning themselves with the government. It was not the coolest decision for someone to choose to become a cop. However, my younger brother, Amos, wanted to be a police officer when we were little boys. He wasn't really encouraged to pursue policing, and in the end, he trained as a fitter and turner and became an auto mechanic.

Interestingly, the flipside of all this resentment toward police officers was a combination of perverse fear and a proud association with the police within certain segments of people in the community. Families of police officers (including all the distant and unknown cousins) would proudly name-drop their connections with police. Imagine the ambivalence police officers had (and still have today) being feared, honoured, disliked, and hated all at the same time.

As children, we grew up in a milieu of unhealthy perceptions toward the police. Obviously, these perceptions were passed on consciously and subconsciously by parents, neighbours, and the community at large. Consequently, they created a culture repulsed by the police, right across the country. You can imagine the unhealthy complexity of the relationship that exists between the police and the people within such an environment.

Zimbabwe got its independence from the oppressive Rhodesia regime on Friday, April 18, 1980. What a day to remember! A new police force, the Zimbabwe Republic Police (ZRP), was inaugurated. Unfortunately, even for ZRP, more than thirty-six years later, their reputation is not exactly impressive. I learned recently that people refer to the ZRP as *Zirema Re Povo*, meaning "the fool of the masses." As you can see, this is not a respectable way to refer to the national police. I guess, just like any other police service around the world, there is a lot of work to be done by both sides to create healthier relationships with the community.

Quite frankly, each of us has countless stories to tell about our experiences with the police and the way policing was done in our different countries of origins, as well as here in Canada. Hopefully, you do share your stories and experiences with others along life's journey.

Another focus of this book is to help us to see that even though our past experiences with the police may have been unhealthy, it is possible to choose to learn to relate to the police in healthier ways. The police also need to learn how to relate to the public in ways that put high nobility in policing. True, not all police officers are created equal; there are some, sadly, who have tarnished the noble career of policing through word or deed. They are human beings with shortcomings and limitations, like all of us. This is not an excuse for their unacceptable misconduct but rather a painful and shameful admission of the high cost for wrong choices and unprofessionalism.

We can choose to learn to relate to each other (the police and the community) in healthier ways than we have done in the past. There are options to do things differently. It is never too late to do the right things. Of course, the police has an important role to play in the facilitation of such relational dynamics.

Chapter Two
Welcome to Canada!
Bienvenue au Canada!

As a little boy in primary school in Zimbabwe, I remember the geography lesson on Canada. I was intrigued by Canada's landscape, particularly the tundra region and the prairies. I recall saying to myself in that class, 'I will go to Canada one day.' For some reason, other parts of the world didn't have such a strong appeal to me. My desire to come to Canada was rekindled while I was a student at Daystar University College in Nairobi, Kenya, as I thought about possible opportunities to further my education. After my return to Zimbabwe, it did not take me long to start searching and considering various Canadian colleges and universities. I used to dream about being a student in Canada—sitting in a class and absorbing information to equip me with life skills to make the world a better place. I still remember the thrill I experienced that day in Zimbabwe when I finally received the letter of admission to study at Prairie College in Alberta. However, my excitement vanished when it dawned on me that I could not go to Canada right away because I had no money for tuition, not to mention the airfare. I began to yearn for the dream to come true.

The application process was tedious because I had to remit funds, little by little. Five years later, I received even better good news. I guess, at some point, the admissions director at the college was convinced that I was serious about studying there. The college graciously gave me a scholarship that helped to meet the tuition balance needed for my first academic year. Basically, I came to Canada to pursue further education. I still remember arriving and getting off the plane at Calgary International Airport on a bright sunny September afternoon. I felt a rather cool prairie breeze, yet everyone else was in shorts and t-shirts. I was cold. I knew straightaway that I was no longer enjoying the African sun. It did not take me long to learn, like many Canadians, that we have four distinct seasons in Canada, and that we can experience them all in one day.

Later, as I attained my educational goals, I began to entertain the thought of staying in Canada. The thought was triggered by the challenge (and reality) of seeking to renew my Zimbabwe passport in time to travel to Manila, Philippines, where I had been invited to be a guest lecturer in Quezon City. I was informed by the Zimbabwe Embassy office in Ottawa, that it would take a long time for me to get my passport renewed in time to travel to the Philippines. It was at that time that I opted to obtain a Canadian passport, since I was a permanent resident by then. I also became more aware of employment opportunities in Canada within my line of training, and hence, decided to make Canada my new home.

In Canada, there are different police organizations (or bodies) and levels of policing. Being the second largest country in the world, one can appreciate the value and practicality of this approach. There is the Royal Canadian Mounted Police (RCMP), responsible for monitoring and overseeing all the federal or national and international police and security matters. Then there are provincial police services such as the Ontario Provincial Police (OPP) or Sûreté du Québec (SQ)—Quebec Provincial Police. There are also tribal police services on First Nations Reserves. Finally, there are numerous police services in towns, municipalities, metropolitan cities, and regions serving our culturally diverse communities across Canada.

Each of these levels of policing are made up of men and women who serve and protect lives and property 24/7, 365 days of the year. York Regional Police (YRP), is one of these police services within the province of Ontario, serving a designated population.

Chapter Three
The Turning Point

After immigrating and settling in Canada, I found myself becoming curious about how policing is done here. Apparently, I had not been aware that there was this underlying fascination and curiosity with the police within me. I could tell from a distance that there were some obvious differences between the police in my native country and the police in Canada. My cultural experiences dictated that I should always keep my distance from the police. You see, from my past experience with police officers, their mere presence (uniforms and cars) were painful symbols of legitimate fear, violence, brutality, discrimination, tribalism, and racism. I dared not to get closer to them.

This mindset reminds me of a comment from one of my friends, a middle aged gentleman from the Caribbean Islands, after he learned that I was a police chaplain. He said to me, "Man, what are you doing hanging out with Babylon like that? (Babylon is slang for police or a corrupt government system). My heart sank upon hearing that, especially knowing that he is a father of young children. I wondered, painfully, what type of a picture of the police he could be painting for his children. Obviously, I do understand why my friend made such a remark with deep emotion. He has been hurt deeply by the police. His experiences in his native country influence his perceptions of the police here in Canada. Unfortunately, he told me that even some of his encounters with officers here have not been cordial or constructive. Those experiences have also contributed to his dislike and distrust of the police. I really feel for my friend. As a friend to both (the Caribbean man and the police), it pains me to see such dysfunction between the police and some members of the community. My friend is not always right because he is human; he has limitations. This is true of the police also; they are not always right because they are human.

Accordingly, I have undertaken to share my perspectives and trigger thoughts through this book in an attempt to find possible solutions. It will require collaboration from both parties to create a different and better relationship between them.

My first time walking into a police station in Canada was at a Royal Canadian Mounted Police (RCMP) detachment in Three Hills - a small town just east of Calgary, Alberta. I needed to have a document certified by the police. I dreaded going in because of my negative experiences with the police back in Zimbabwe. However, that experience was an eye opener for me. I walked out of that station with a rather positive attitude. The encounter was thoroughly professional, and, to my surprise, my fears about the police dissipated. Now, in hindsight, I wish that RCMP detachment had an open house for students, especially knowing that there are many international students who attend the college across the street. I can still hear the joking remark from Paras, a fellow international student from Trinidad, when he saw me coming out of the police station. He shouted, "Oh no, Francis, what did you do again this time?" We both had a good laugh. However, the implication was that only people in trouble with the police go there. I wonder how many other international students thought this way and would have concluded the same about my visit.

My educational journey took me to a few colleges and universities across Canada. Fast forward to when I later moved from Alberta to British Columbia (BC), then drove from BC to Ontario. I lived in Ottawa for a few years while attending university there, in Ottawa, and then moved a little west to a small community called Arnprior, before moving to York Region in the Greater Toronto Area. On arrival in York, it did not take long to see and experience that it is, indeed, one of Canada's most culturally diverse communities. Every day, I passed by the police station to and from work. Then one day, I saw this big portable sign by the side of the street advertising an open house at the station. Now, that caught my attention and interest. I knew right away that this was a great opportunity. I decided I would go that Saturday in the summer of 2003. I wanted to check out the station, tour the premises, and learn more about the police in Canada, especially within my own neighbourhood.

The day finally came. I showed up at the police station early enough to observe the preliminaries and hoped to watch from a safe distance. What a big surprise it was, seeing myself walking into a police station! True, there was considerable ambivalence within me as I walked through the front doors, as I did not know what to expect. At least I was not the only one in attendance. There was a rather long line up of people waiting for something, but I didn't bother to ask what it was. My eyes were attracted to a table displaying pamphlets and manned by uniformed police officers, both male and female. Something also caught my eye: I observed that there was cultural diversity on that team of police officers. Since I did not know anyone there, I found it easier to simply walk over to the table, hoping to look through the information on display.

I was surprised to find out that the officers were friendly and welcoming. I was even more surprised when one extended a handshake along with a smile that appeared quite genuine. If my memory serves me well, I think I ended up shaking hands with the rest of the crew (the platoon) at that display table. After picking up some information pamphlets, I asked one of the officers, "Does York Regional Police have police chaplains?" The officer paused a bit and replied, "That is a very good question, sir. I don't know the answer. However, the chief of police is here, and I can take you to ask him directly." I responded promptly, determined to shake this off. "Oh no, there's no need for me to go to the chief for that. I was just curious. Don't bother; no sweat." The officer was not aware of how his innocently helpful offer had created such turmoil and discomfort within me. I thought, "*Me, going to talk to the chief of police? There is no way I am going to converse with such a high-profile person.*" The officer interrupted my thoughts as he stepped out from behind the information booth. "Sir, come with me. I will take you to the chief right now." Again, I tried to turn down the invitation but the officer was extremely cordial. I followed him reluctantly.

I followed the officer beside a winding line of people. It then dawned on me that this was the same line I had noticed when I first arrived at the police station. People were lining up to meet and greet the chief of police. The officer just waited for the chief to finish the conversation he was on when we arrived, then he got the chief's attention and graciously spoke to him. "Excuse me, Chief, this gentleman was asking if we had... uh, what was that you were asking about, sir?" "I was asking if the police has chaplains," I responded promptly. The chief and I shook hands and he said, "That is a good question, but as you can see, today is a very busy day and we cannot really visit and chat about that. Would you have a business card to leave with me so that I will get in touch with you?" I pulled out my wallet and handed him my business card. He took a quick look at it and asked, "How do you pronounce your last name?" I was delighted to help him say it correctly. Being a person with an eye for detail, he also noticed the few initials after my last name and asked what my postgraduate studies were in. After the brief conversation, he said, "Thank you, sir. I will be in touch." I walked away with a big grin, thrilled that I had actually met the chief of police.

Two weeks later, lo and behold, I received a phone call from his office inviting me to arrange an appointment to meet with him. I was pleased and quickly made arrangements. However, between the time of the phone call and the set appointment, I began feeling butterflies in my stomach and wondered if I had made the right decision to agree to go to the police headquarters to meet the chief. All my fears, concerns, and insecurities about the police had resurfaced, bombarding me left, right, and centre.

The day came and I went to the police headquarters. I received a warm welcome at the front desk and was directed to the chief's office. We went past a few floors in the elevator and a row of doors. I still recall my first impressions of that office upon entering. First, it was quite spacious. It was also very neat and organized; everything seemed to be in its rightful spot. Finally, it had a welcoming atmosphere created, I guess, by the person behind the desk, whom I had first seen just a little over two weeks before. He immediately stood up to welcome me. His sheer height, stature, and style of expression would have an overpowering effect on anyone, but I must hasten to mention that his cordiality dissipated all my fears and concerns about the police, not to mention my trepidation of being in his office. His people and communication skills helped me to feel at home and relaxed. As we chatted, I couldn't help but visualize the weight and complexity of the responsibilities on this person's shoulders.

The chief provided me with pertinent information about the state of the police chaplains program, and his overall vision for it. He asked me candidly, "If we were to give you an opportunity to become one of our police chaplains, what would be some of the key duties and responsibilities that you would undertake?"

I thought it strange to question my suitability before giving me a job description. It seemed my response to that open-ended question must have met his expectations, and of course he gave me the job description afterward. I was thrilled at the end of that visit—really an interview—to hear Chief Armand La Barge say, "York Regional Police is happy to extend an invitation to you to join our ranks as one of our chaplains. Congratulations!" Indeed, this was something I had yearned for and hoped would happen. I was delighted. That beautiful summer afternoon of 2003 saw me begin a new journey and the process of getting enlisted as a chaplain with York Regional Police. I completed the required paperwork made arrangements to get measured for my uniforms, and exposure to protocol, procedures, and basic training in safety and other aspects of policing. This was a great day for me, and it still feels like it was just yesterday. The rest is history.

Chapter Four
The Value and Role of Police Chaplains

Policing in the western world is very different from policing in developing countries. However, the truth remains that police officers worldwide are a special breed of people with a special calling to serve and protect others. On the other hand, police chaplains are also a special breed of people called to come alongside and serve police officers in ways that facilitate and enhance policing. One might think of chaplains as people with a ministry of presence, insofar as they can only be as effective to the degree to which they show up and rub shoulders with the police officers and staff.

In addition to their theological/religious and professional training, police chaplains are sworn in by a judge, taking the oath to serve and support the police with a high degree of confidentiality. They receive training in basic safety, protocol and procedures, wearing the uniforms, understanding the chain of commands, and more. A chaplain's rank may vary, as determined by the chief of police or commissioner. In York Region, police chaplains hold the honorary rank of inspector. This is a high rank at the senior management level. Other police services or police jurisdictions may give chaplains a different rank depending on where the chief of police wishes to place them within the organizational structure.

Generally, police chaplains have a dual role. First and foremost, they serve police officers, support staff, and their families. Second, chaplains also serve the community as ambassadors for the police. The job description of most police chaplains would include the following:

1. Be available on-call to respond to requests for emergencies, like on-the-scene crisis intervention and management of such situations as suicides, attempted and threatened

suicides, death notifications, officer's injury, or death in the line of duty;

2. Be available to support police officers and their family members at funerals, engagement parties, wedding ceremonies and receptions, and housewarming (or new house blessing) events;

3. Be available to ride with patrol officers responding to calls, and assist officers and citizens as needed;

4. Be available to officers wanting to chat or in need of guidance, or different forms of spiritual, psycho-spiritual, emotional, or relational support;

5. Be available to respond to citywide or regional critical incidents in partnership with other emergency responders attending to the needs of victims or their families;

6. Be available to participate in ceremonies such as police college graduations, in-house graduations, memorial services (the most solemn of all police gatherings), workshops, conferences, special events such as dinners and fundraisers, and other special assignments as requested;

7. Be available to participate in community events like citizenship ceremonies, cultural events, prayer breakfasts, communal sports, and youth engagement initiatives in schools;

8. Be an ambassador for policing in the community and beyond;

9. Be an ecumenical representative of the police within a culturally and religiously diverse community.

Although the chaplains may be of a particular religion or belief system, they are there to serve all people in the police service and the community, regardless of demographic, race, ethnicity, gender, sexual orientation, religion/no religion or spiritual background. This includes officers, their families, and other people from all walks of life. It is important for chaplains to be ecumenical and work to serve all people.

As you can see from these defined duties and expectations, there are numerous activities and opportunities available to keep chaplains occupied in the police organization's activities. The chief or commissioner, as the organization's commander, envisions, designs, and directs the service's activities and culture. As a result, not all police services have chaplains, nor do they all place equal value on their role and significance. Some chaplains are more visible and active participants in their respective teams than others. In some circles, chaplains can be under-utilized if the chief (or designate) has not made time to discover the distinctive value and role they bring to the organization. Some police chaplains have tremendous skills, education, work, and life experiences, if tapped into, would contribute remarkably to effective policing and community engagement initiatives.

Generally, there are at least two categories of police chaplains, depending on the workplace culture or environment as determined by the chief of police and the command team of that police service.

The first are chaplains who participate in various duties, responsibilities, and services within the police service upon request. These are very good chaplains who show up and participate in the life and events of the police service when called upon.

The second are chaplains who participate in those same duties, responsibilities, and services within the police service, and who go beyond the basic expectations. These chaplains take initiatives, enquiring whether they could be of assistance at upcoming events, or they simply show up at events (provided there are no limitations to seating arrangements). These chaplains choose to visit the police stations every now and then to connect with the troops and staff, for the purposes of building and strengthening friendships. They can also come up with down-to-earth ideas that create and enhance opportunities for participation and involvement.

These chaplains may also request to be present from time to time at "parade" briefings that take place before the officers begin their shift and at special meetings. The chaplains' involvement largely depends on the freedom given to them by the chief, or prior arrangements put in place by the senior command team. On the other hand, creative chaplains who take initiative and have a deep desire to engage in the life of the organization are a real blessing to the police service. The police service is a large enough organization with various departments and units to allow chaplains to serve numerous officers, support staff, and their families.

However, given the nature of the duties and responsibilities of chaplains, there are countless expressions of their ministry of presence that go unnoticed or do not need to be noticed due to aspects of confidentiality. Indeed, much of what chaplains do, never hits the headlines, yet they contribute remarkably to the health of the organization. The truth is, well-organized police services help their chaplains to function creatively within the organization by providing the freedom to participate at the parades unannounced, or to ride along on patrols (provided they show up ahead of time and in full patrol uniform, and connect with senior command team representatives on duty). The key for chaplains here is to display their interest to connect and establish meaningful friendships with officers and support staff at all levels. Chaplains would be wise to actively invest in friendship building if they desire to be effective. Effectiveness is a by-product of healthy relationships.

Dallas Theological Seminary's distinguished Professor of Education and Leadership, Dr. Howard Hendricks, said, quite profoundly, "If you wish to impress people, do it from a distance; but if you wish to impact lives, do it from close range." When a chaplain is known within the organization as a friend, and knows officers by name, rank, and responsibilities, it opens numerous windows of opportunity to serve, and ultimately increases the chaplain's distinctive value.

Indeed, it is this second category of chaplains, those who engage and participate in the life of the police family, who impact lives at deep levels. The connections and levels of impact and influence that emerge from within such friendship environments are powerful, engaging, transformative, deep, and long lasting. It is no surprise, then, that the chaplain who engages at this level is often invited to places where the officers hang out, provides counselling, facilitates conflict resolutions, makes referrals to other professional resources within or outside the police organizations, officiates weddings of officers and their friends, participates in housewarming parties or house blessings, birthday parties of officers and their friends, and connects and chats with officers even during off-duty times, both in-person and online. These connections and behind-the-scenes services may never hold the spotlight of the chief's monthly bulletin board or the newspaper headlines, but they will achieve the primary focus and motivation of being a true friend to the service.

Some Points to Ponder

1. For the chief / the commissioner of police / police leaders:

   a. In order to develop an active and effective chaplain program or unit, consider engaging the professional services of a highly qualified chaplain who will serve as the coordinator of chaplaincy on a full-time or part-time basis. Police services that have created this coordinator position have enjoyed tremendous benefits, infused new life, and built active participation of their chaplains. Such a position would allow the coordinator someone skilled and experienced as a police chaplain (a practitioner)—to provide experiential knowledge, leadership, and oversight to the chaplaincy program with a spiritual and religious touch and high degree of professionalism.

   b. Police chaplains seem to be among the most under-utilized professionals in some police organizations. There would be wisdom in making time to uncover the untapped resources and skills within your team of chaplains, and structure the unit accordingly. Open consultative dialogues between the police chief (or designate) and the chaplains could unearth numerous ideas that could set new directions of chaplaincy program in motion. Intentionally including chaplains as part of the professional team for member care has numerous huge benefits for the police organization. They are both "insiders" and "outsiders" of police culture - which may give them an upper hand when it comes to connecting with the officers and support staff.

   c. There is wisdom in creating a clearly defined job description with measurable and realistic expectations for chaplains. Such a document provides mutual understanding and agreement between the police and the chaplains, thus establishing clear lines of communication and accountability. The professional skills of the coordinator would be a great asset in creating and facilitating those open dialogues.

d. Intentionally increase the value and visibility of chaplains (as part of the holistic approach to member care) at various events and functions within your organization. By constantly highlighting their role within the police family, you display their professional value and significance as an integral part of policing with the community.

e. Design and create ongoing professional opportunities and requalification procedures for the chaplains. Considering that police officers and staff participate regularly in refresher courses. Similarly, the chaplains would benefit from all efforts to help them sharpen their professional skills.

2. For the police chaplains:

a. In consultation with the chief (or designate) or the chaplains' coordinator, creatively increase your visibility and involvement. Intentionally make time to connect, frequently, with the police (the command team, senior officers, frontline officers, and support staff). If you happen to be in the neighbourhood of the police station or headquarters, drop by to say hello. Be a proactive professional who values the "ministry of presence beyond structured times and events."

b. Be an inclusive and ecumenical chaplain in your involvements. Remember, you are the chaplain for all people with no regard for creed, faith, religion (or no religion), race, colour, et cetera. Make everyone feel comfortable around you.

c. Aspire to become a true friend. Build friendships, earn their trust, and earn the right (and privilege) to be heard as a friend who also happens to be part of the team. Take initiatives to connect with police officers from other police jurisdictions - and show support for what they do. Officers have great appreciation for those linked to police organizations … "there is a family connection."

d. You would be wise to ensure that alternative dispute and conflict resolution skills are among your additional valuable skills and training in your toolbox.

e. Value and maintain an active membership with the Canadian Police Chaplain Association (or a comparable professional body) and participate regularly in their specialized professional development opportunities.

f. Retain a teachable spirit, always looking for opportunities to advance yourself holistically. Police officers periodically go for in-house requalification. Let the chief, commissioner, or training branch know that you wish to participate in activities that would increase your knowledge of policing and enhance your services as a chaplain. It is always a wise disposition to see yourself as a life-long student.

g. Yes, religion is very powerful. It shapes the very core of people's identity. It is important for people for bear in mind that healthy relationships lead to national patriotism not ethnic nationalism. National patriotism is about national pride - strong alliance with other citizens expressed through love and devotion for your country. Ethnic nationalism, on the other hand, is about a shared heritage based on faith (religion), culture, ethnic ancestry, heredity, descent or kinship. As you can see, national patriotism is very inclusive while ethnic nationalism is exclusive.

h. Therefore, our commitment as people committed to creating healthier relationships in our communities, should be to national patriotism, especially considering our commitment to multiculturalism. As Canadians, we are strategically placed (constitutionally/by law) to create such a powerful display of cultural mosaic which can be the envy of the world. Let us work together to create healthier relationships.

Chapter Five
Life on This Side of the Atlantic Ocean

Let me hasten to declare without hesitation that Canada is the world's greatest country in which to live! I know that I am biased. I admit it, but this is a type of bias I am proud to embrace wholeheartedly and hold up high.

Of course, Canada is not a perfect country. Sadly, we have a painful history with our friends the indigenous peoples—the First Nations, Métis, and Inuit. This has resulted in what I would call Canada's worst unresolved conflict, a topic deserving its own book. It is encouraging to note that collaborative efforts are being made to bring healing. Though Canada is not a perfect country, it is a perfectly good country!

Of course, our police services and police officers are not perfect, but they are perfectly good services, and perfectly good officers!

Of course, we have our own social/interpersonal ills and issues at various levels—municipal, provincial, and federal.

BUT we are a great nation, *eh?*

Canada constitutionally adopted multiculturalism in 1970, affirming the value and the dignity of all citizens and residents regardless of race, ethnicity, language, or religious and non-religious affiliations. Indeed, Canada's multiculturalism embodies our fundamental belief and practice that "all citizens are equal before the law." The Canadian citizenship, Constitution, and Charter of Rights all guarantee everyone's freedom and dignity, enabling citizens to retain their cultural identities and to unapologetically take pride in their ancestry. Multiculturalism in Canada is about integration, not assimilation. *Integration* is the process of incorporating as equals into a society or cultural environment. In this process, one retains their cultural characteristics, though over time there will be a cross-pollination of cultures, resulting in volitional changes or adjustments among communities. *Assimilation*, on the other hand, is the process of embracing and acquiring social and psychological characteristics of a predominant society or cultural environment. One is basically 'swallowed up' by the receiving society. Where an assimilation mindset exists or is expected, chances for an outsider's survival can be slim if there is no intentional and rigorous adaptation to the prevailing culture's customs and attitudes.

Obviously, those choosing to make Canada their home are expected to embrace the laws of the land, abide by them, and consciously engage in the process of identifying and selecting Canadian values. These will assist their integration process so that they can participate in the nation's social, cultural, economic, and political affairs. This is one reason I appreciate the active role that York Regional Police plays in organizing citizenship ceremonies in cooperation with cultural centres, community centres, and other organizations. I am also pleased that York Regional Police now holds these ceremonies in the atrium at police headquarters, thus intentionally creating opportunities to invite new immigrants and the culturally diverse community at large, to the police building. This, in my view, is a strategic move that facilitates the overcoming of perceived barriers or boundaries. Indeed, these activities create wonderful opportunities for police to interact with new citizens, thus helping them to overcome interpersonal barriers and build friendships that contribute to healthier working relationships.

As mentioned earlier, Canada is a great country, but it is not perfect. Its multiculturalism represents an admirable philosophy whose practical application can be very complex. Canada's multiculturalism embodies what my friend Mike Noble of Navigators Canada describes as "the neatness of philosophy and the messiness of reality." Multiculturalism creates its own varieties of complications, challenges, and opportunities. All human beings have underlying complex worldviews, opinions, expectations, beliefs, and supporting behaviour. While these realities cannot be legislated or enforced by law, the police are there to help secure cultural harmony within the confines of the constitution and human rights.

As immigrants to Canada, we all go through tremendous adjustments and changes in our efforts to settle in our new home country. For some of us, the process is rather smooth, while for others, it is difficult. In any case, in addition to bringing our diverse skills and qualifications to contribute to Canada's economy, we also bring our cultures with us. Naturally, they greatly influence our perceptions, behaviours, and how we relate to others around us.

In his book, *Making Peace*, my friend Dr. Jim Van Yperen defines culture as "a complex system of assumptions, practices, stories, and beliefs that guide how a common people think and act as well as what they value."[4] Observation and experience lead us to conclusions about people and facts, often without adequate or correct information about who or what they really are. We often interpret things, situations, and information from limited perspectives, and this can lead to unhelpful conclusions. As you know, if we do not seek to obtain the right information or if no data are provided to us, we often fabricate our own information, arriving at conclusions about what we would have observed and creating a "truth" that is in fact little more than personal opinion. Sadly, we often raise our personal opinions to the level of non-negotiable truth. We blindly perceive our preferred perceptions to be the only true way of looking at things. We forget the reality of having written the script, not realizing that we can re-write it and even create new information, leading to totally different conclusions if we access and analyze the right information.

An Australian friend, Yassim Abdel-Magied, says that our unconscious biases are to be "identified, acknowledged, and mitigated against"[5] if we desire to have healthier relationships with others in society. These biases and assumptions are culturally and experientially formulated. Surprisingly, the "truth" with any assumption about other people is that once you establish that assumption, it seems every behaviour and form of communication displayed—verbal or non-verbal—confirms your bias and assumption all the time. Confirmation bias is a subtle and powerful reality. In fact, pre-judging is a survival tool for many of us in society. Once we develop a theory about a person's

---

[4] Jim Van Yperen, Making Peace: A Guide to Overcoming Church Conflict. Chicago: Moody Publishers, 2002, p. 28.
[5] Yassim Abdel-Magied, TED Talks: December 2014, Brisbane, Australia.

disposition or behaviour, everything we observe is processed through the lens of confirmation bias. For example, if one's experiences with the police in their country of origin were not positive, every time they encounter a police officer, their biases and assumptions emerge. Sadly, they will perceive and relate to the officer through their own experiential and acquired knowledge and culturally designed lenses. When it comes to culture, there are some realities we need to be aware of:

1. **Culture** is complex.

2. **Culture** is created by human beings who have limitations, and therefore is not perfect.

3. Every **Culture** has both good and bad elements. No culture is perfect.

4. **Culture** constantly changes. It is influenced by many factors within itself as well as through interaction with other cultures around it.

5. **Culture** is learned. We pick it up from birth and continue learning right through life's journey as we adapt to our different geographical and socio-economic environments.

6. **Culture** provides a worldview that gives us the theoretical foundations, influencing how and what we observe. It guides our interpretations of life's events.

7. **Culture** shapes behaviour. We act from our cultural makeup, perceptions, interpretations, and wealth of life experiences.

8. **Culture** has subtle nuances and realities. Expressions of our culture come out visibly, invisibly, and as second nature without conscious effort.

Indeed, culture is complex. It is into this complexity of culture that the police are called to serve. Policing itself has a culture: (a) in relation to itself (that is, how it perceives, understands, or defines itself); and (b) in relation to its community, its region/county, or the people it serves, insofar as the carrying out of its duties and responsibilities in a given locale or context are concerned. As you can imagine, each police service or department develops ways of doing business in accordance with its comprehension of the environment it serves. Society has created a culture with some expectations of what the police should be, do, and not do.

Today, the police serve in culturally diverse communities across the nation. Such milieus make policing an onerous task. Unfortunately, given our past experiences with the police from different jurisdictions around the world, officers in Canada sometimes become reminders of oppressive and ruthless governments and political entities and systems. Police uniforms and cars can be viewed as symbols of unscrupulous government regimes. Therefore, it would require intentionality and jumping through numerous interpersonal hoops (by both parties—the police and the citizens) if real positive changes resulting in healthier relationships, harmony, and better communication are to be established.

There are major differences between policing in Canada and the West, and policing in developing countries. Here are a few worth noting:

1. In the Canadian context, neutral descriptive titles like "police officers" are used rather than "policemen" or "policewomen" to circumvent distinctions of gender and to carry our intrinsic value of equality among officers. Similarly, the title "firefighters" is also used in place of "firemen."

2. In Canada, the police seek to intentionally engage in collaborative policing approaches through 'policing with the community.' Establishing healthy working relationships with citizens is a priority for police services, in the belief that to be an effective organization, they must collaborate with their communities. This explains why there are Neighbourhood Watch programs to facilitate good policing efforts in many communities across Canada. Apparently, in some police jurisdictions around the world, the police operate differently. They police the community on their own, with or without intentionally seeking to collaborate or build healthier working relationships with their communities. As a result, the presence

41

of the police officers in the community, for the most part, is not well received by the people. Instead, it creates suspicion and tension.

3. In Canada, we refer to the police organizations as 'police service,' not 'police force.' Basically, what they provide and how they provide it is summed up as a service and it is done within a context of "serving their communities." "Service" and "serving" reflect an ethic of care, and people expect the police to show care for their well-being. This is why people tend to speak out whenever the police seem to display any sense of uncaring. In fact, people have the right and the means to file complaints against the police. In other jurisdictions around the world, police organizations are commonly referred to as 'police forces' in the community. Indeed, the words we use to describe the police reflect our perceptions and our expectations of them, as well what they do or are supposed to do. The words we choose to employ depict the populace's underlying views about how the police relate to the community. Thus, referring to the police as "a service" or "a force" provides two totally different starting points for defining this relationship.

4. In Canada, there is a high degree of accountability structure. Police are constantly under the scrutiny of the public eye as they carry out their daily duties and responsibilities. We live in a world where everyone with a mobile phone is a 'potential journalist or reporter.' In addition, there are different ways to register complaints against the police for those believing they have been treated unfairly, or who perceive any form of questionable behaviour or speech pertaining to police interactions with the public. A complainant can provide the facts or details of the incident to the police service online (some now have apps available on mobile phones), or by walk-in to the police station. Such information is taken seriously and evaluated by senior staff and the command team, unless it is some trivial or unfounded attempt to spite the police. In either case, complaints are tallied, reflected in the annual community report, and archived at the end of each year. In addition, if someone ends up hurt or killed in the course of an encounter

with the police, an independent civilian organization called the Special Investigation Unit (SIU) is called to investigate so that the police are not caught up in the potentially compromising situation of investigating themselves. In some other jurisdictions around the world, police are not accountable to the public, but to themselves. They make, enforce, and break the rules at will, without any repercussions or sense of accountability. Such environments breed disorder, distrust, an unhealthy fear of the police, and in most cases, corruption.

5. In Canada, professionalism is highly valued in policing. Most police services would list "professionalism" as one of their core values. You see, it goes without saying that how the police present or presence themselves in the community either earns or undermines their privilege to be heard as effective professionals. For example, the York Regional Police motto is "Deeds Speak." In other words, "Actions speak louder than words." The agency believes that what you do demonstrates what kind of a person you are. This principle is applicable to both the police and the citizens. Officers, in particular, are held to such high standards of behaviour with regards to how they display the vision, the mission, and the values of their organization in order to maintain credibility with the public. In other jurisdictions, professionalism is not always a core value, even though it may be written down as such.

Sometimes, sadly, police officers are perpetrators of corruption, racism, discrimination, and other vices that undermine what they purport to stand up for. As a result, these police have lost at least two qualities essential for effective policing: respect and trust from those they should be serving and protecting from harm.

6. In Canada, due process and rule of law are exercised within an unwavering commitment to be guided and evaluated by human rights and social justice. The way the police carry out their responsibilities is governed by the Canadian Charter of Rights and Freedoms, legislation, and the Universal Declaration of Human Rights. In situations where civilians feel that their human rights are violated or compromised by

police, there are established processes allowing citizens to be heard. Superintendent Ricky Veerappan (who heads the York Regional Police Diversity, Equity, and Inclusion Bureau) noted, "Police must speak the language of human rights, and their actions must demonstrate that." This overt commitment to the application of human rights conveys a powerful symbol of community-based policing. This approach is not shared by some jurisdictions around the world because there is little or no serious commitment to abiding by human rights standards. In some contexts, the police abuse their power and authority, and violate the human rights of those they are supposed to serve and protect. Furthermore, officers who violate human rights, break the law, manipulate rules, and mistreat civilians are not disciplined, punished, or reprimanded severely. Trust and confidence in the police is lost. Consequently, the citizens have legitimate fears about the police; they fear for their lives at the prospect of being at the mercy and disposition (if not disposal) of such unscrupulous and un-accountable bullies.

7. There are also salary differences. In Canada and other developed countries, police officers are paid well compared to other countries around the world. Currently, a York Regional Police cadet-in-training starts with a base salary of $55,126. After qualifying, within approximately four months, the new officer (police constable) moves to 4th Class Police Constable ($67,905), and then progresses toward 1st Class Police Constable ($100,421). Generally speaking, the officer would move from 4th Class to 1st Class within about year, with re-classification on the annual anniversary date. With all such possible vertical and horizontal mobility, the cadet-in-training this year could potentially become the chief of police in few decades' time.

Officers also receive extended health coverage including dental, optical, prescription medications, pension, paid vacation, education reimbursement, semi-private hospital care, travelling health insurance, life insurance, long-term disability coverage, and insurance in the case of accidental death or dismemberment. Coverage is extended to their spouse or partner and dependents, beginning on the first day of employment.

As you can see, there are several noticeable differences between the police in Canada and other jurisdictions around the world. However, the bottom line is that all police services (and police forces) around the world respond to disputes and conflicts 365 days of the year. Day in, day out, each shift presents frontline officers with numerous challenges that need to be resolved. The approaches used by the various police jurisdictions separate the effective from the ineffective – 'policing with the community or policing the community' police services (or police forces) around the world.

Chapter Six
The Four-fold Engagements of Effective Policing

As I see it, the bottom line is that police services exist to create, enhance, and maintain law and order. They enforce the laws in the nation.

In my sixteen years of experience as a police chaplain, I have provided various services in different contexts – in the community and within the police organization. I have come to the conclusion that effective frontline policing consists of four primary intentional involvements, among others: (1) Community Engagement, (2) Crime Prevention, (3) Law Enforcement, (4) Alternative Dispute and Conflict Resolution, Mediation, and Negotiation. These four intentional engagements (in no order of priority) are inseparable for any police service seeking to engage in effective policing in any jurisdiction.

I was pleased to learn that the law governing police services in Ontario—*Police Services Act*, 2018, S.O. 2018, C. 3, SCHED. 1—highlights six core declarations of policing: (1) Ensuring the safety and security of all persons and property in Ontario, (2) Safeguarding the fundamental rights guaranteed by the Canadian Charter of Rights and Freedoms and the Human Rights Code, (3) Cooperation between the providers of police services and the communities they serve, (4) Respecting victims of crime and understanding of their needs, (5) Sensitivity to the pluralistic, multiracial, and multicultural character of Ontario society, and (6) Ensuring that police services are representatives of the communities they serve. Indeed, the fundamental focus is on effective policing.

It is encouraging to see that these six declarations zero in on the relational aspects of policing, which is the hallmark of effective policing and the main thrust of this book. The fact that our police services in Canada (and specifically in Ontario) are regulated by such clearly defined principles, allows for transparent and ongoing community-driven evaluations of the police. Notwithstanding the real challenges and limitations of policing within our multicultural Canadian context, the police in Canada stand out as leaders in the world.

Furthermore, the Police Services Act declares, 'Policing shall be provided throughout Ontario in accordance with the following principles:

1. The need to ensure the safety and security of all persons and property in Ontario, including on First Nation reserves.

2. The importance of safeguarding the fundamental rights and freedoms guaranteed by the *Canadian Charter of Rights and Freedoms* and the *Human Rights Code*.

3. The need for co-operation between policing providers and the communities they serve.

4. The importance of respect for victims of crime and understanding of their needs.

5. The need for sensitivity to the pluralistic, multiracial and multicultural character of Ontario society.

6. The need to be responsive to the unique histories and cultures of First Nation, Inuit and Métis communities.

7. The need to ensure that police services and police service boards are representative of the communities they serve.

8. The need to ensure that all parts of Ontario, including First Nation reserves, receive equitable levels of policing.'

Again, we see an indisputable commitment to effective policing expressed philosophically and relationally. These are the declarations and principles that guide our police services in Ontario, and across our nation of Canada.

However, one of the grave limitations of our western world is that, given the high value and focus placed on specialization, we tend to run the risk of polarization, categorization, isolationism, and overlooking the inter-connectedness of life. Strictly speaking, life is a unit. Therefore, there is value in employing holistic, harmonized approaches in the efforts to provide variety of services and meet the real needs of people in our diverse communities. Hence, these four engagements of policing need to be embraced and placed together as a unit to create, enhance, and maintain law and order in society.

Community Engagement

Chief Eric Jolliffe of York Regional Police has produced an excellent document on community engagement for his Master of Arts in Leadership degree at Royal Roads University titled "Enhancing York Regional Police's Relationship with Its Visible Minority Communities," (March 2012). It is encouraging to observe that the chief, especially given his role as the commander of a police service, has intentionally invested time and countless resources in producing such crucial research. It surely speaks volumes to have the chief carry out such specialized community-focused research aimed at finding out how best the police can connect and build healthy relationships with the community. This is commendable.

Chief Jolliffe rightly defines community engagement as "giving individuals a voice and involving them in decisions that affect them, their community, and their neighbourhood," (p.21). This is a well-rounded and loaded definition of community engagement. In view of this definition, Chief Jolliffe suggests specific elements the police need to engage the community, such as having broader community engagement strategies, educating both police and community members, addressing police culture, engaging members at all levels of the organization, and addressing its operational capacity. The fundamental thread that weaves in and out of all these elements is 'relationships.' It goes without saying that developing healthy relationships, both within the police service and between the police and the community, is the foundation for creating harmony and fertile soil for effective policing.

In chapter four of his research project, Chief Jolliffe presents four conclusions essential for developing and "enhancing relationships with visible minority communities." Although his research is aimed at improving relationships with visible minority communities, the data and insights are applicable to everyone in the community, regardless of ethnicity, country of origin, or cultural distinction. His conclusions are insightful, introspective, and convincing, and they display a teachable spirit on the part of the police, even though they are in a position of authority. He highlights the following ingredients for healthier relationships, namely: (1) Broader community engagement that fosters a climate of collaboration and trust; (2) Education of both the community and the police are critical elements of relationship building; (3) Police culture needs to be addressed to sustain healthy community engagement; and (4) Community trust and confidence can be gained by engaging all levels of the organization.

These ingredients need to be embraced by any police service that desires to engage in effective policing and make a positive difference in the community as intentional non-negotiable realities. In other words, the effectiveness of the police in serving the community is equal to the depth of community engagement they choose to settle for. Indeed, it is a symbiotic relationship that must be handled with great care. Thus, when there are serious expressions of disputes and conflicts between the police and the community, the approaches employed to resolve the disputes and conflicts will reflect the depth of friendship between the two parties, including how well they really know and respect each other.

True, there are times when small expressions of disputes or misunderstandings can surface between the police and the community. However, if the relationship is healthy, all attempts to resolve issues would be processed and handled without the airing of dirty laundry in public, through the media or otherwise. Such attacks in public reveal unhealthy relationships between the police and the community, and they should be addressed through "learning conversations/dialogues."[6]

---

[6] Douglas Stone, Bruce Patton, Sheila Heen. Difficult Conversations: How to Discuss What Matters Most. Penguin Books, 1999. All three authors are distinguished lecturers at Harvard University.

Some Points to Ponder:

1. Regular forums for open dialogues between the police and the community could be established to create opportunities to establish, develop, and maintain police engagement in the community. These meetings could be held in the community room at the police station, the community centre, in a school hall, or some neutral rendezvous.

2. Educational opportunities could be created for the police to enhance on their understanding of community engagement.

3. With community engagement being one of the key pillars of effective policing, police services with a community engagement mindset will contribute remarkably to world-class policing.

Crime Prevention

One of the key pillars and regular habits of effective policing is crime prevention. This involves intentional and incessant efforts to combat, reduce, deter, and prevent crimes in the community. Although there is always great value in regular patrols—increasing police visibility and presence in the community—crime prevention goes way beyond flying the police colours. In fact, it marks the difference between police jurisdictions that are fighting crime (putting out fires) and those that also proactively engage in preventing crime. In other words, any police service that creatively and intentionally puts the right resources, the right officers with the right heartbeat for people in crime prevention will, most definitely, be effective.

Such an approach to policing and crime prevention involves a variety of factors and intentional approaches such as creatively making time to educate residents/citizens, community organizations, businesses, and schools on crime prevention and self-defence tactics. Again, the bottom line is intentionally engaging the community. In other words, when the police collaboratively work closely with communities and local organizations, strong partnerships are created, thus contributing to crime prevention and solving crimes. Such healthy relationships make it difficult for criminals to engage in their illegal activities. Neighbourhoods and businesses feel much safer in such contexts, as opportunities for crime are reduced markedly.

Therefore, an effective police jurisdiction exists to proactively reduce, deter crime and criminals, and thwart opportunities for crime. This can only happen when the police creatively and intentionally engage the community. Healthy relationships are essential and key to crime prevention approaches because police officers are viewed as friendly and approachable professionals.

Some Points to Ponder:

1. Sessions or gatherings initiated and conducted by the police to educate citizens on crime prevention matters could be frequent occurrences. True, criminals try to do their homework to stay ahead of the police, but the truth is, the police are a lot smarter. Set up periodic opportunities to inform good citizens about tips on how to recognize crime or criminal trends.

2. Intentional collaborations with community partners could be an ongoing and integral part of policing with the community. Key stakeholders could be identified and invited into "learning conversations"[7] on strategic crime prevention efforts and pursuits.

3. With crime prevention being a non-negotiable engagement of effective policing, there would be value in creating a police culture that highly values an intentional crime prevention mindset and practices.

Law Enforcement

Effective policing involves law enforcement; that is, ensuring that the laws of the land are respected and obeyed by everyone. The police exist to enforce the law by intentionally seeking to discover and deter crime, respond to the choices people make, and investigate those

---

[7] Douglas Stone, Bruce Patton, Sheila Heen. Difficult Conversations: How to Discuss What Matters Most. Penguin Books, 1999. All three authors are distinguished lecturers at Harvard University.

members of the society who violate the rules and norms established by the government. They also professionally prepare official documents (reports of their investigations) for courts so that better and healthier relationships are established in society. By the way, it is not the police's role to humiliate, correct, rehabilitate, or punish those who violate the law; that is the responsibility of the courts.

There are at least two types of violators. The first are those who violate the law intentionally or deliberately. Unfortunately, and sadly, some people are purposefully bent on breaking the law. These individuals know the consequences of breaking the law, yet they go ahead and do it anyway.

True, there are many factors that contribute to such a disposition in life. However, such an utter disrespect for the law and law enforcers (police officers) is a disheartening reality in society. Just to imagine that there are some people who decide to violate the law, endangering their lives and the lives of others, is so inhumane.

The second group are those who violate the law unintentionally or ignorantly. True, there are times when good law-abiding citizens may break the law, perhaps forgetting or failing to do the right thing because they are in a hurry. For example, in Ontario, a good citizen may forget to renew his/her expired vehicle validation sticker for the licence plate due on your birthday, or forget to renew their driver's licence on their birthday (generally renewed every five years). Generally, there are a few days' grace period for the vehicle validation sticker, and even for the driver's licence renewal. Some people may also fail to bring their vehicle to a complete stop at a four-way stop sign or a flashing red light. However, bear in mind that ignorance is not an excuse for violating the law.

Police officers are government representatives (guardians of the law) authorized to maintain order and ensure public safety while obeying the law themselves. If a resident or citizen has violated (or deemed to have violated) the law, the police's responsibility is to investigate the matter thoroughly and with professionalism, and lay charge or not. When a charge is laid, the police must then prepare the documents (deemed evidence package) for the courts so that the judges, the legal interpreters of the law, will make a ruling on the matter. This is why in Canada, everyone is innocent until proved guilty in court. However, police must treat everyone professionally and with courtesy, dignity, and respect at all times. Failure to uphold those principles or the police code of ethics creates unhealthy relationships between the police and the members of the community. Indeed, healthier relationships between the police and the community are always fertile soil for safe and peaceful communities.

Some Points to Ponder:

1. Creative ways, along with stiffer fines, could be introduced by the courts for those who continue to violate the law (especially those who violate the same laws). The police would then enforce such laws.

2. Police officers who issue fines or tickets to violators of the law within a friendly environment or conversation are generally well received by the recipients, even when the members of the community know that they are in the wrong. Therefore, there is wisdom in officers displaying professionalism and a spirit of caring when they enforce the law.

Alternative Dispute and Conflict Resolution, Mediation, and Negotiation

Frontline police officers are constantly engaged in dispute and conflict resolution and mediation. Inspector Anil Anand with the Toronto Police Service defines policing as "the state's response to controlling and dealing with public conflict within societally defined norms."[8] Although this definition of policing is loaded, effective policing is much more than this. In effective policing, the police officers are presented with numerous opportunities to amplify their humanity through public service for public safety. Superintendent Ricky Veerappan of York Regional Police is correct when he says, "First and foremost, police officers are champions of social justice

---

[8] Inspector Anil Anand, Toronto Police Service "Lecture on Policing" York University, summer 2014.

54

and human rights." Such an understanding of policing carries a much broader scope of policing than the 'notions of controlling and dealing with public conflict within societal defined norms.' However, an analysis of Inspector Anand's definition narrow in its scope, leads to the conclusion that there are at least five realities that emerge from it:

1. The police are representatives of the government, not of a political party.

2. The police ensure that the people abide by the laws of the land.

3. There are norms and standards for everyone to live by that are chiefly created by the government. Those norms are legislated by process rather than whimsical expressions of someone's preferences. They come from laws, rules, and regulations passed by government.

4. Those norms and standards form civic boundaries applicable to everyone in the land, including police officers. At police college, trainees learn to translate, explain, and enforce the norms, standards, and laws to the citizens they serve.

5. The police officer's job includes, among other things, crime prevention, responding to and managing public matters, and resolving disputes and conflicts related to how people conduct themselves (in speech and deed) according to socially defined norms and standards.

Police officers are conflict resolution, negotiation, and mediation practitioners. This is the total of frontline policing: interacting with people to resolve interpersonal relationships and helping people on a daily basis to abide by the laws of the land. This is why I strongly believe that police officers' performance reviews or evaluations should include their people skills. These components are beyond the standard approaches based primarily on statistics generated from activities as depicted in submitted reports. Performance evaluations could also include healthy balances of both *qualitative measurements* such as crime-preventative approaches applied, disputes and conflicts and mediations dealt with (or resolved), aspects of educating the public, acts of caring for the people they serve, important lessons learned, et cetera; and *quantitative measurements* such as arrests, convictions, warnings, tickets, traffic stops, important lessons learned, et cetera. They should also include peer and platoon supervisor evaluations.

Furthermore, careful observations of the annual crime statistics compiled and published by Statistics Canada, which are based on data provided by police services across Canada, indicate without a doubt that frontline police officers are dispute and conflict resolution and mediation practitioners. The police-reported crime statistics in Canada (2017) along with the related Crime Severity Index (CSI) reveal that criminals are not slowing down. In fact, there is evidence that frontline police officers are constantly engaged in dispute and conflict resolution, and mediation. Police stats show us various crimes that are committed: property crimes (*breaking and entering, frauds, thefts, and arsons*), crimes against persons (*homicides, attempted murders, sexual assaults, robberies, uttering threats, threatening phone calls, assaulting police officers, impaired driving charges*), drug charges, and non-criminal (*attempted suicides, mentally ill cases, missing persons, mischief, vehicle collisions, criminal and non-criminal traffic violations*). Evidently, these crimes reveal that police officers are dispute and conflict resolution and mediation practitioners who prevent crime, fight crime, enforce the law, resolve disputes and conflicts, and mediate in countless and diverse situations.

In addition, a look at the various departments within most police services' organizational charts, in the light of the statistics compiled and by Statistics Canada, seem to highlight and confirm, also, that frontline police officers deal with various forms of disputes and conflicts on a regular basis in the course of carrying out their duties and responsibilities. For example:

- **Patrol Units** respond to calls for various services, vehicle collisions, suspicious persons or vehicles, property crimes, 911 calls, traffic infringements, confirming that vehicles and drivers are roadworthy, et cetera.

There are two important pieces of information regarding **911 calls in York Region**:

1. Every **911 call is "a priority call"** and is attended to by at least 2 units (or 2 officers); and

2. Someone in a life-threatening situation can discreetly dial 911 and hang up without speaking to dispatch. This is called the "**Silent 911 Call.**" Units will be dispatched immediately to that location. I once used this service in a real life-threatening situation and was very glad I'd known about it. When "my friends" showed up, I was delighted and relieved. Of course, these important services are used strictly for emergency purposes only. A misuse of these services is costly because it results in tying up police officers who could otherwise be useful in situations needing real help.

- The **Commercial Motor Vehicle Safety Unit** inspects vehicles to ensure safety on the roads. Some people take their chances and put unsafe vehicles on the road hoping that they won't get caught putting their lives and the lives others in danger.

- The **Corporate Communications (Media Relations Unit)** liaises with media regarding major incidents or crimes, making sure that the public is provided with timely and accurate information. Some people are confrontational, and MRU officers have to handle such situations with tact and professionalism.

- The **Marine/Underwater Recovery Unit** helps efforts to recover missing property or missing people and helps keep the public safe on the water.

- **Canine Units** employ police service dogs to chase down or track criminal suspects, hold them while the officer arrives, track missing people, and play integral roles in apprehending individuals who have committed serious criminal offences. They are also used to locate evidence of a crime such as weapons or clothing, for searching or locating illegal drugs, explosives, cadavers (corpses or human remains), or just guard an area (like a jail/prison) to keep suspects from escaping. These police dogs assist officers in maintaining order.

- The **Diversity, Equity, and Inclusion Bureau Unit** cultivates healthy relationships with people, ensuring that members of the community live in harmony within our culturally diverse environments. This unit also resolves conflicts and disputes related to hate crimes, bullying, et cetera.

- The **Traffic Bureau** ensures that vehicles are roadworthy and that drivers operate their vehicles safely. Traffic safety is always a top concern for police and citizens alike. The bureau enforces compliance with laws on distracted driving; combating seasonal increases in drunk driving; car racing in the summer; as well as ensuring drunk drivers are are kept from getting behind the wheel, kept off the roads, and are assigned sober designated drivers.

- The **Emergency Response Unit (ERU)** is the tactical team that engages in and de-escalates situations where dangerous weapons are reported to be present. In some cases, lethal weapons, armoured trucks, robots, and other devices can also be used to de-escalate situations whilst attempting to resolve serious conflicts, disputes, or life-threatening circumstances.

- The **Fraud Unit** investigates and combats different types of frauds (in-person, electronic, etc.) to ensure that citizens and residents are not being preyed upon, manipulated, or taken advantage of by con artists.

- The **Human Trafficking Unit** ensures freedom of movement for all people without being enslaved or forced to engage in illegal activities or in any activities against their will.

- The **Child Pornography and Exploitation Unit** investigates and monitors activities surrounding the exploitation of minors for pornographic purposes. These children are lured and exploited by some people who should know not to engage in such activities that abuse and dehumanize such innocent lives.

- The **Guns and Gangs Unit** ensures that dangerous and illegal weapons are kept off our streets and out of the community. In most cases, this unit also works in collaboration with the drugs unit because guns, gangs, and drugs often go together. Unfortunately, some citizens engage in buying and selling dangerous and illegal weapons to support territorial gangs and their activities.

- The **Homicide Unit** investigates circumstances surrounding suspicious deaths using forensics and other specialized and high-tech tools to determine causes and circumstances. Homicides reveal the presence of unresolved disputes and conflicts.

It appears that frontline officers are constantly engaging in resolving disputes and conflicts in the community, dealing with people who are not only in dispute or conflict with each other, but with government laws and regulations. Of course, there are other duties and responsibilities police officers carry out besides the predominant engagement of handling disputes and conflicts.

If dispute and conflict resolution and mediation or de-escalation techniques are paramount to effective policing, it becomes expedient to ensure that specialized training in alternative dispute and conflict resolution, negotiation, and mediation or conflict de-escalating training, are intentionally included in police colleges and academies as core courses, as well as within their respective in-house police services. Not only should these be a primary focus of training, but also become part of the ongoing professional development and requalification process. Police organizations that periodically equip their officers to sharpen their alternative dispute and conflict resolution, negotiation, and mediation (de-escalation) skills will contribute remarkably to effective policing in their communities.

On one hand, given the nature of the various situations arising regularly in the course of policing, the use of force may be applied. There are times when the use of force is warranted as part of law enforcement. Police officers are adequately trained on the application of force. There is an intricate and complex internal process an individual officer would go through before applying force. This is part of professional training in the use of police equipment. For example, the Ontario Use of Force Model starts with *officer presence* (non-verbal skills, body language, position in the room or outside in the open, listening skills, proximity to subject, facial expressions, eye contact), *verbal communication skills* (opening words, active listening, use of questions, tone, volume, and speed of voice, choice of words, politeness), and then followed by *choice on the tool to use in a given situation.* Similar models are also advocated and used by the National Use of Force Framework. This is a difficult and complex topic because situations and responses do not always follow the script. This is why we (the police and the community) need to dialogue about all this. I may not know enough to provide a solution but I want to learn how to find solutions to the issues that affect us. You may not be equipped or qualified to exegete all this, but the point is that there is value in learning how to articulate and clarify the process that helps to build trust between police officers and members of the community.

Indeed, the police ought to be in an intentional disposition to make verbal communication and the accompanying non-verbal communication as priority tools or methods to engage and invite people into "learning conversations."[9] The use of force should always be a last resort taken after applying verbal communication skills and techniques to resolve an issue. It is one thing to say something like this as an outsider, and quite another thing to say or do something from the perspective of a police officer within a potentially explosive situation. It is not always easy for a police officer to engage solely in dialogue without thinking about the use of force, especially when there is a slight chance of potential danger to the public or the officer.

The use of new lingo would be helpful here as we seek to create new and intentional approaches to alternative dispute and conflict resolution culture within police organizations. Instead of "use of force" concept, perhaps new nuances with regards to 'conflict resolution tactics' or 'de-escalation tactics or equipment' could be introduced. There might be wisdom in moving away from the 'use of force' notions in order to help officers to begin to see their equipment from the different angles of 'peace making / peace keeping.' Such an approach would facilitate a new mindset driven by compassion and humility as key components of excellent quality service delivery.

To help change the relative primacy of force versus verbal engagement, the community would have to work hard to dispel some of the negative perceptions the officers may have about

---

[9] Douglas Stone, Bruce Patton, Sheila Heen. Difficult Conversations: How to Discuss What Matters Most. Penguin Books, 1999. All three authors are distinguished lecturers at Harvard University.

the community. Based on previous experiences, there are some very real and justifiable fears that police officers may have about certain types of people in the community (especially those bent on being on the wrong side of the law). By the same token, some people in the community may have justifiable fears about police based on previous experiences. One of the wisest responses to someone's expression of fear is to acknowledge it, rather than ignore or challenge it. It is not your responsibility to approve or disapprove someone's feelings, but instead to show a degree of empathy by acknowledging their feelings. In addition, engage the individual in a 'learning dialogue' to find out how they arrived at such feelings. After hearing their story, help them to analyze and process the feelings for the purpose of evaluating, discussing, and informing them so that they consider some options in the light of newly provided information. It is fruitless to argue about whether the feelings are baseless or justifiable.

As alternative dispute and conflict resolution practitioners, there is greater value in frontline police officers sharpening their conflict resolution skills (people skills) so that they become better and more effective in carrying out their duties and responsibilities in our communities. The key focus here is that police officers need to be equipped with alternative dispute and conflict resolution skills, including the ability to detect aggression, either existing or potential conflict, and de-escalate situations without the use of force, if it is not warranted. Such dispositions don't just happen. They are products of ongoing intentional specialized training that ultimately becomes second nature for the officers in the course of carrying out their duties. Furthermore, such training develops officers who are highly committed to excellent quality customer service approaches that are steeped in humanity—friendliness, courtesy, respect, and peace keeping. It produces an officer with what some practitioners have termed *emotional intelligence*—"someone who understands himself or herself and can understand emotions evoked during the job and manage their emotions effectively. They understand the emotions of others and are able to use emotions to create positive encounters."[10] Emotional intelligence has a framework of five elements: self-awareness, self-regulation, motivation, empathy, and social skills (*Emotional Intelligence*, Daniel Goleman, 1995).

---

[10] McShane, Steven and Kevin Tasa. Canadian Organizational Behaviour. McGraw-Hill Ryerson, 2017, pg. 105.

Within the context of seeking to establish healthier relationships, such a disposition would help to accomplish at least three realities:

1. It has potential to facilitate "learning conversations"[11] and opportunities to dialogue because it encourages being interested in other people's lives, and this case, the people the officer interacts with in the course of carrying out the job.

2. It has the potential to allow the police officer to share or display qualities that reveal humanity. People are attracted by real stories. One young man once said that cops with a heart to help people make a difference in people's lives, and they hold their egos in check.

3. It has the potential to equip or pre-wire the police officer with the ability to connect with members of the community in amicable ways, without speaking or behaving combatively.

Some Points to Ponder:

1. If frontline policing is predominantly community engagement, and it is, then skills in alternative dispute and conflict resolution, mediation, and negotiation should be a fundamental piece of police officer training.

2. Police officers with excellent people skills have greater chances to contribute to effective policing with the community.

3. The police recruiting process could ensure that the cadets and new recruits possess either the potential ingredients for or the basic understanding and value of negotiation skills for healthy relationships.

4. The annual re-qualification training could also include aspects of people skills as part of officer professional development.

---

[11] Douglas Stone, Bruce Patton, Sheila Heen. Difficult Conversations: How to Discuss What Matters Most. Penguin Books, 1999. All three authors are distinguished lecturers at Harvard University.

5. The annual officer performance evaluation could include specific aspects on how the officer relates to and gets along with others, as observed by peers, support staff, and senior management, along with the usual aspects defined and reviewed by the police organization.

6. Complaints filed by groups or individual members of the community against the police organization or individual officers could be analyzed or evaluated with transparency, preferably by neutral practitioners. This proposed process would facilitate the building of trust and a healthier relationship between the community and the police.

7. Remember, generally speaking, whenever there is a dispute or a conflict between the police and the community (or a police officer and member(s) of the community), both parties would have contributed to that situation, either directly or indirectly.

8. A willingness to dialogue openly (by engaging active listening skills) with regard to what transpired helps to bring better understanding between parties. The contribution to that dispute or conflict might have been initiated by a gesture, demeanor, verbal or non-verbal communication, a behaviour interpreted as suspicious by the observer, et cetera.

In conclusion, the four intentional ingredients of effective policing highlighted in this chapter are (1) Community Engagement, (2) Crime Prevention, (3) Law Enforcement, and (4) Alternative Dispute and Conflict Resolution, Mediation, and Negotiation. Although these four fundamental realities of policing are police initiated, they cannot be realized without the voluntary collaboration of the community. In other words, the effectiveness of any police service is directly proportional to the depth of friendships and strength of partnerships established in the community being served. Such symbiotic relationships have great potential to enhance the humanity (ubuntu notions) within each of us and benefit our interactions towards healthier relationships.

Therefore, the police have the gigantic and complex responsibility to invest various resources in studying the community through "learning conversations,"[12] engage the community, and establish healthy relationships before inviting the community into strategic dialogues for the betterment of the police and the community, respectively.

Indeed, the community as a whole, as a major stakeholder, has an important role to play in this process. Intentional collaboration with the police is a fundamental non-negotiable ingredient for safe communities. Policing does not happen in a vacuum, but in a specified and defined context. Both the police and the community need to voluntarily collaborate with each other to develop healthier relationships and safer communities, and to enjoy mutual benefits.

---

[12] Douglas Stone, Bruce Patton, Sheila Heen. Difficult Conversations: How to Discuss What Matters Most. Penguin Books, 1999. All three authors are distinguished lecturers at Harvard University.

Chapter Seven
Some Challenges to Effective Policing

Like religious leaders, police officers serve at least four types of people:

1. People who like them; the ones who think the world of them and believe that police are wonderful people that the world cannot be without; those who say that the police should receive good salary increases periodically, because they deserve it;

2. People who dislike them, wonder what they really do, and why police should even be paid "that much money" when they don't do much. Ostensibly, these individuals seem to find fault with police services and officers in general, and usually have only negative comments to say about them;

3. People who are indifferent and seem to care little about what they do or don't do. "Who cares?" or "I don't give a damn," they would say, while expecting immediate assistance or service whenever they need it;

4. Lastly, those who intentionally work against police, undermining what they do or stand for. These people routinely violate the laws of the land and our societal norms, and engage in criminal activities that impact communities negatively, corrode society, and deliberately undermine the police.

Let me borrow the three-pronged expression used by the York Regional Police, which helps the organization to evaluate their philosophy and operational strategy:

- Vision – *Inspired*

- Mission – *Focused*

- Values – *Driven*

These three pillars are intricately connected and influence each other in remarkable ways. In fact, each facet emerges from the other and becomes an expression of the other.

The truth is, policing does not occur within a vacuum. Police actions and methods of operation are supposed to reflect the fundamental ethos of their organization. Of course, daily life brings both the expected and unexpected, and each day is unique with regards to the nature and content of calls or situations to which police respond.

Here are a few of the challenges I believe police officers may face on a regular basis, in no particular order of value:

Listening to Stories

Officers are constantly listening to testimonials from citizens, and this is not always an easy exercise. Quite often, officers get to hear what we think they should hear. In their book, *Difficult Conversations: How to Discuss What Matters Most*,[13] Harvard University's trio, Stone, Patton, and Heen show that our stories are different because we all have different pieces of information available to us, different observational skills, different interpretation abilities (mainly due to our different past experiences), and of course different self-interests, which lead us to totally different conclusions.

Now, imagine how challenging it is for officers to decipher our stories while processing their own stories in the midst of the dialogue. Not only would the officers need to have specialized training in active listening skills, but they also need to have tremendous curiosity and interest in relating to each individual appropriately and professionally. Excellent interpersonal communication skills are non-negotiable for officers.

---

[13] Douglas Stone, Bruce Patton, Sheila Heen. Difficult Conversations: How to Discuss What Matters Most. Penguin Books, 1999. All three authors are distinguished lecturers at Harvard University.

Police officers spend a lot of time telling stories about their policing experiences. Their stories are coloured heavily by their available information, their observations, their interpretations, and their conclusions. Although there is a desire and commitment to remain professional and objective, the truth of the matter is that subjectivity surfaces and influences the story telling process. You can imagine how the stories are told in the end.

Officers tell their policing stories in at least four different ways. First, there is what I call the "**inline perspective**." This is the telling of their stories through their official reporting channels such as their radio systems, notebooks, verbal reports to supervisors and senior management team, and in the courts. Second, officers share their stories through what I call the "**online perspective**," carried out casually in regular day-to-day conversation as they go about their duties and responsibilities with their peers. This is a relaxed environment where stories are told mostly for entertainment, without any serious sense of accountability in narration. Third, officers tell their stories through what I call the "**offline perspective**," opening up and telling stories to trusted individuals (family and friends), and sharing stories with a high degree of caution. These are censored stories with the "inline story" details intentionally left out. Here, the officers feel a bit safer to narrate their stories, but without interfering with confidentiality. Lastly, officers tell stories about their policing through the "**intra-line perspective**." This perspective is about the individual officer telling policing stories to 'self.' Storytelling from the intra-line perspective is powerful and complex, influencing one's cognitive processes, choice of words, tone of voice, non-verbal expressions such as gestures and body language, and feelings. What officers do on-duty or off-duty reflect their worldview, that which provides a theoretical and practical framework to give meaning to their life experiences. Daily responses in given situations are reflections of their intra-line perspective, the internal voice. This is the most intimate, most powerful, and most influential level of communication for a police officer. This internal voice will determine the response and action of the officer in a situation based on the story or stories being told to 'self.' In other words, all the police college training, in-house training, coaching officer training, and years of experience on the road, including childhood experiences, all find their value, meaning, and expression through the intra-line perspective.

Officers must pay careful attention to this internal voice and not ignore or suppress it. They must dialogue with it, inform and educate it so as to tell "self" what to process and how to process, thus ultimately influencing the behavior consistent with the calling to be a police officer. Neglecting this internal dialogue can lead to internal conflicts and costly outcomes, and sometimes to insurmountable turmoil. Indeed, this is why our officers are to be given ongoing specialized training, guidance, and coaching in this area. They can serve more effectively when their thought processes, activities (responses), and feelings reflect the stories they are telling the 'self.' In other words, police officers determine what they think, what and how they feel, and what they do as they carry out their daily duties. The words and actions of a police officer can make them a hero or a zero in a split second as per their response to the intra-line story.

Intercultural Realities

The world is now a global village. Everywhere you go, you find people from different countries with divergent cultural expressions. By virtue of creation by God, everyone has a right to live and interact with others. Consequently, our cultures cross-pollinate and we end up with expressions of other cultures in the way we do things. The culture triangle, as explained by Blaine Donais of the Workplace Fairness Institute, has ideas, structures (hidden), and behaviour (observable) that shape our lives in remarkable ways, even as we generally observe actions and behaviour without seeking to understand the underlying influences that lend them meaning.

Canada is constitutionally committed to multiculturalism and its related cultural complexities, even as we are practically unclear as to what this multiculturalism is. I guess there is truth in the saying, "You cannot articulate what you cannot define." Someone once said that 'when you deny a problem, you can't address it.' Each of us needs to remain humble enough to admit that we do not really know what multiculturalism is and be willing to learn its practical implications and how to relate well to others in this intercultural conglomeration.

Indeed, culture is complex. One of the best comprehensive definitions of culture I have come across is by Dr. Desmond Ellis, a professor who teaches conflict resolution at York University. He says, "Culture is a set of enduring meanings, values, and beliefs that characterize national, ethnic, gender, and other groups, and orient behaviour."[14] Obviously, these enduring meanings have been transmitted across generations for many years within each cultural group. Someone has also said, "Culture is, basically, that sum total of the learned way in which people live."[15] This definition is loaded and there is a lot to unpack. Yes, the culture we find ourselves in shapes our worldview and behaviour, both theoretically and practically. By the same token, police services/jurisdictions are to continue to evolve - adjusting their 'police culture' in order to increase their effectiveness in the communities where they serve.

In multiculturalism and inter-culturalism, we wrestle with a mix of individualistic and collectivistic realities. Individuals within the community are responsible for their actions and represent unique cultural realities of their communities.

Here are at least six such realities we deal with as we interact with each other on a daily basis:

1.   Self-identity

This is who you are, how you perceive yourself, and how you relate to everyone else and the world around you. Ultimately, self-identity is the sum expression of the stories we tell our selves about ourselves. Whenever someone does something to you that affects your self-identity either negatively or positively, it goes deep in your heart. A lot of our conscious and sub-conscious assumptions, prejudices, judgmental attitudes, labelling, and so on, reflect our perception of self.

This self-identity can be individual or collective.

[14] Professor Desmond Ellis, ADR Lecture: York University, spring semester 2014.
[15] www.answers.com

Since we each have a past, our self-identities with respect to policing have constant downloads from previous experiences involving police. Those experiences influence how we relate to people or to our situation. As police officers encounter a vast mix of people with self-identities formed over an even more diverse mix of experiences, complex and unpredictable outcomes are to be expected. Police officers have a daunting task as they relate professionally to people in the execution of their duties. When a police officer's words or deeds touch upon a person's self-identity—either negatively or positively—it goes deep into the soul of that person. In addition, any previous encounters or interactions with a police officer (including those from my country of origin) play into the current context and either enhance or undermine communication, affecting outcomes of the dialogue. As individuals, members of the public also do and say things affecting the self-identity of police officers. This is why both parties need to be mindful of their words and actions as they can profoundly impact the self-identities of each other, negatively or positively.

It is possible to unlearn bad habits and to embrace modes of communication that help build healthier relationships between the police and members of the community. It does, however, take both parties to make the relationship work.

2. *Diversity*

In a global village, we have people from various countries of the world in every nation; communities within communities. Diversity is a reality nearly everywhere, especially in major cities. Our various police services would, therefore, be wise to reflect the community's cultural diversity in their recruiting processes, officers' in-training, and senior officer ranks. Police ought to be intentional about reaching out to, acknowledging, and embracing the cultural diversity in their community. Placing a high value on other people, especially those who look different from us, is not always a natural progression or reality for most of us. This is about accepting other people as equal co-habitants of this world. It is about putting value on all people, regardless of their ethnicity.

Strictly speaking, we are all ethnically diverse; no ethnic group or race is better than the other. It is when one people group believes and behaves like they are superior to others that discrimination and racism surface and create conflict and disharmony in society. Police actions and interactions relate directly to realities of mutual inclusion, value, and respect. Although Canada's cities and towns pride themselves on cultural diversity, police services often fail to reflect that in their ranks. The Canadian Broadcasting Corporation (CBC) surveyed police services across Canada on racial diversity and found that there's still much work to be done in this regard, (CBC News Survey: May 2016). Only the Halifax Regional Police was found to be as racially diverse as its community. All other police services across the country showed that there is room for improvement towards reflecting their cultural diversity of their respective communities. We hope the statistics have changed remarkably, for the better, in the past three/four years and beyond. Those statistics reflect on the great need to adjust police culture right across our nation. Imagine the sociological and relational impacts such lack of cultural representation can have on the community.

If our police services desire to earn the respect and trust of their communities, it would be wise to lead by example with regards to realities of diversity and inclusion. Citizens do notice when the police service does not reflect the community's diversity, and that can raise issues of representation/misrepresentation and bias in people's minds. Failing to address matters of diversity and inclusion can create further tension as well as mental and social barriers between the police and the people.

In addition to dealing with realities and challenges of inclusion and diversity in the community, police also deal with inclusivity and diversity within their own organizations. Therefore, there would be great wisdom in offering refresher courses to help officers sharpen their social skills within culturally diverse contexts.

You have heard it said, "If you aim at nothing, you will hit it all the time." For a police service to be effective while reflecting its community's cultural diversity, there ought to be a strong value attached to diversity; otherwise, they get stuck in appeasements, insincerity, cosmetic adjustments, show biz, and tokenism. It is always easier to maintain the status quo than to chart a new course of direction.

3.   *Practices*

The multiculturalism in communities across Canada implies an assortment of practices. Cultural practice is created by people as a way of coping or adjusting to their specific environment, and Canada's laws, indeed, honour and espouse many of the land's cultural practices.

Interestingly, people often retain a practice whose value may be long forgotten or lost in the maze of life. For example, you may have heard the story about the bride preparing a ham dinner in the kitchen. When her husband asked why she had chopped off the ends of the ham before putting it in a tray, she said, "Honestly, I really don't know why I did that. All I know is that Mom used to do that every time she cooked a chunk of ham." They asked her mother, who responded, "I don't know why I chopped off the ends, but I'd watched my mother do it every time." When Grandma was finally asked, she answered, "Back then, we had a small oven with a small tray. I had to chop the ends off so the ham would fit."

Canada being a land of immigrants (except for the First Nations, Inuit, and Métis), some values and practices from our countries of origins may find themselves in contradiction with the norms and laws in Canada. The "rule of thumb" notion on practices—having broad applications with no strictly accurate and consistent interpretation—does not work within the rule of law contexts. Therefore, if unsure whether those imported practices contravene local laws, citizens would be wise to check them out with their local police, since the best practice is to embrace the laws of the land and abide by them.

4.   *Experiences*

Our responses to life's situations reflect conditioning from prior experience, and the experiences individuals have had with police influence how they relate to police today, or tomorrow, unless that individual has worked to improve behaviours and mental states. One's opinions of police impact their behaviour in police presence, influencing how they speak and joke about police when in conversation with family and friends.

By the same token, a police officer's experiences in various contexts with individuals in the community have subconscious and conscious influence on how the officer relates to other members of the community, associating through age, race, gender, clothing, type of car being driven, et cetera.

The bottom line here is that healthier dialogue about past experience can do at least two things for us. First, it brings a better understanding of the individual, especially the process that led to the conclusions they have embraced (What happened?). Second, it opens opportunities to create new paths for the future. Both parties—the police and the public—are key players in this and should ask, how can we create a better future together?

5. Perceptions

By "perceptions" we are referring to mental impressions, ability, or the process of knowing or interpreting things through our senses. Our perceptions express a long and complicated process shaped by life experiences, both the good and the bad. In other words, every response we make, whether it is a comment, simply silence, or body language, is deeply and intricately connected to how we perceive the situation and those involved. These perceptions are developed through personal and shared experiences, interactions, and stories over long periods.

Our perceptions of police are all learned. By the same token, police perceptions of people or the community are also learned. As you can imagine, when you bring the police and the community together, both parties have established perceptions of each other over time. The power of perceptions and preconceptions should never be underestimated. Once an individual has a perception of the police, they will, more often than not, appear to confirm those perceptions. This will also be true of police perceptions of individuals or communities. When a police officer has a preconception about an individual, whatever the individual does will appear to confirm the officer's preconceptions. In other words, our preconceived ideas about other people always seem to play tricks on our minds, leading us to judge, label, and anticipate behaviour that corresponds to and concurs with our assumptions.

Learned, developed, and nurtured over time, these perceptions become our reality in our subconscious systems. If the perceptions are of a negative nature, the interaction between parties is filled with tension, and potentially unhealthy communication.

One way to deal with negative or unhealthy perceptions—be it of the police officers or an individual member of the community—is to create opportunities for dialogue, specifically "learning conversations."[16] Both parties need exposure to information that will assist in the process of learning and unlearning about each other.

This mindset or disposition cannot be developed on the spot but rather within the confines of ongoing conversations.

6.   *Building and Maintaining Healthy Relationships*

Healthy relationships are key to effective policing anywhere in the world. Without them, human behaviour is affected and dysfunction sets in. Examples of such dysfunction include violence, distrust, corruption, abuse of power and authority, bullying, suspicion, harassment, abusive language, threats, intimidation, posturing, cynicism, keep your head down syndrome, low morale, dissatisfaction, undermining leadership, deceit, high degrees of fear, power imbalances, among other social pathologies. Basically, poor communication will be evident. Healthy relationships do not happen without a deliberate, lifelong process requiring effort and cooperation from all concerned parties.

At least three crucial relationships need to be healthy to realize effective community policing: police governance, police family in-reach, and community out-reach.

---

[16] Douglas Stone, Bruce Patton, Sheila Heen. Difficult Conversations: How to Discuss What Matters Most. Penguin Books, 1999. All three authors are distinguished lecturers at Harvard University.

Governance

Each police service has a governing board. In Canada, except in the case of the Royal Canadian Mounted Police (RCMP), these governing boards include civilian members of the community selected to be members. Since we place high value on community policing in Canada, we surely hope that the RCMP will see the value of including civilians as part of their governing board. Though this notion would constitute a new direction, such a move would help build better relationships with the public across our nation. Incidentally, the Canadian Broadcasting Corporation reported in May 2017 that the RCMP's Civilian Review and Complaints Commission chair, Mr. Ian McPhail, had sternly called for the federal government "to introduce civilian governance of the national police." Although this is an individual opinion on this matter, there might be value in considering such a notion to weigh the merits and possible positive contributions to policing. Indeed, such a move has potential to contribute additional benefits toward Robert Peel's notions of "the police are the public, and the public are the police; the police being only members of the public who are paid to give full time attention to duties which are incumbent on every citizen in the interests of community welfare and existence."[17]

For police jurisdictions with civilians on their governing boards, it goes without saying that unhealthy relationships within these boards will affect police operations, public perceptions, behaviour, and actions of police officers as they serve and interact with the community.

In Ontario, the Police Services Board (PSB) oversees all the municipal police services. The composition of the board would include chiefs of police, four members appointed by the regional municipality, and three members appointed by the Province of Ontario. In fact, under the Ontario's *Police Services Act*, "the board ensures that effective and efficient police services are provided to the citizens and residents living in our increasingly diverse and rapidly growing communities. As civilian representatives of the public's interests, the Police Services Board is committed to excellence in community-based policing and police governance. The Board recognizes challenges to law

---

[17] Robert Peel. Quotes@BrainyQuote.com/quotes/robert_peel_260231 (1800's)

enforcement created by a changing environment, demographic shifts, emerging technologies and evolving crime trends and patterns."

Indeed, the PSB's role is crucial to linking the police organization, the chief of police, and the community. There is wisdom in inviting members of the community to observe meetings, or to attend special PSB presentations. Some PSBs do that. This helps to facilitate the citizenry support needed for effective policing with the community.

When the police service is in an unhealthy working relationship with its governing board, dysfunction rears its ugly head in different forms. In some jurisdictions, these may include (or lead to) unconstructive comments about each other in (or via) the media, evidence of poor mutual support such as work-to-rule demonstrations, go-slow approaches, taking their frustration out on the public, or absence of motivation or pride in policing.

Some Points to Ponder:

1. To be effective, increase trust, and build healthier relationships with their communities, police services should consider having governing boards composed of openly selected citizens by the community. This would reflect the integrity of the selection process, thus building trust with the community.

2. Police Services Board (PSB) members should represent the composition of the community in race, culture, colour, gender, expertise, etc. Such reflections or indications of inclusivity further build trust with the community.

3. In the interest of transparency to the community, the qualifications, selection, criteria, and process for PSB members should be clearly defined, published openly, and the members should be chosen or appointed with no sense or impression of symbolic efforts to select individuals from underrepresented groups, simply to portray equality.

4. In the interest of accountability, PSBs could provide reports to the community on a regular basis, with opportunities for

feedback or dialogue with the community.

5. Members of the Police Services Board are key players in ensuring that the board is perceived to be reputable and that it earns the trust and support of the community.

6. The relationship between Police Services Board and the chief or commissioner is critical to the police service operations and how it is perceived by the community. It is necessary that this relationship be healthy. Should tension and conflict develop between these two, an independent dispute or conflict resolution practitioner could be engaged in seeking to resolve the issues. When such conflicts spill over to the public domain, they undermine policing and create community distrust in the police service. Policing is a noble calling and should be treated with high degrees of ethics and professionalism.

Police Family In-Reach

Police organizations are similar to the military in structure and operation. Positions, titles, and ranks of individuals are strictly respected within chains of command.

Given this work culture, relational dynamics with regards to different perspectives and perceptions can sometimes foster tension and conflict. Though the organizational structure has well-established channels for dealing with such matters, it may not be easy, in some cases, for people to use internal procedures for fear of the possible practical implications. Indeed, it can be difficult for junior officers to express different opinions to a senior officer unless there is good rapport between them. Officers are human beings, first and foremost, with feelings and perspectives that need to be acknowledged (not necessarily accepted), then integrated into the execution of duties and responsibilities. The alternative is to sweep unresolved conflict under the rug, resulting in the unfortunate possible effects on the morale and conduct of officers within the organization, as well as their ability to relate effectively to people in the community. As our police officers are professionals providing essential services to our communities, we would expect them to maintain such professionalism despite ongoing issues at the office and in their personal lives. However, let us remember that officers are human beings with feelings, just like anyone else.

Some Points to Ponder:

1. There might be wisdom in including occasional training on relational dynamics by qualified conflict resolution practitioners (like skilled police chaplains - who already have some knowledge of police culture -- or other outside specialists) during professional development or requalification sessions.

2. Develop an ongoing commitment to healthy working relationships, keeping short accounts with one another within the police organization. Merely posting organizational charts and claiming open-door policies won't necessarily produce the desired results. We need systems that actually work for our members. Healthy relationships don't just happen. They require intentionality, hard work, and skills.

3. Engage the services of qualified, reputable, and independent workplace fairness analysts from time to time to assess the relational health and dynamics within the police organization. We cannot leave desired outcomes to mere chance.

4. In the event of officer conduct requiring disciplinary measures, internal investigations by the police tribunal should always be supplemented by an independent tribunal investigating what would have transpired. Police organizations should seek outside input and perspectives in order to secure the public's trust. They cannot rely solely on internal investigations. Results of independent investigations should be disclosed to the community. This makes a powerful statement to the public about the humanity of police officers, the police organization, and their desire to police in collaboration with the community.

5. The mental, emotional, social, physical, and spiritual health of police officers should always be a top priority of police organizations because officers function from the position of their holistic wellness. Since life is one whole, multifaceted unit, there would be wisdom in caring for the officers from such a holistic approach to life. In fact, compassion fatigue, workplace trauma, mental, emotional, spiritual, social and physical wellness ought to be on the radar constantly. Considering that police officers are often first responders on many life-threatening situations, crises, hostages, automobile collisions, deaths, suicides, et cetera - seeing such horrific images can affect their lives holistically and drastically..

Community Outreach

Effective policing is a result of teamwork. Healthy relationships between police and communities take time and require intentional strategies. Unfortunately, in many cases, police jurisdictions are at a disadvantage with regards to trust matters because of public perceptions based on previous experiences and stories from the media. The media has a critical role to play in society. However, there is value in seeking to provide a healthy, balanced perspective on the police. Needless to say, police have no control over the public's perceptions but they can certainly help change them by intentionally doing and saying things that contribute to building trust in the police. Remember, "deeds speak."

The notion of policing in partnership with the community is indispensable today. The police cannot effectively serve the citizenry without collaborating with them. When there is mistrust, a social or relational chasm is created between the police and the community. Consequently, the police are called names and given numerous labels like "bullies – who are quick to apply the use of force on every little expression of resistant behaviour by any member of the public," as one anonymous young man chose to put it. Personally, although I am disappointed when I hear such comments, I also view these as potential opportunities to bridge relational gaps. No wonder I get pumped up with the thought that the police can intentionally and creatively help to alter these perceptions and negative labels. True, some of our police officers have, disappointingly and regrettably, done or said things that have made it difficult for communities to trust and collaborate with police. However, the large majority are great officers who are true to their calling and committed to the high professionalism and ethics of protecting and serving our communities and country with unwavering pride.

The commitment to policing with the community is widely embraced by police organizations across Canada. Even our federal police, the RCMP, talks about "bridge-building"[18] in their vision for effective policing. In the words of the RCMP, "To achieve our goal of safe homes and safe communities, we must build and maintain strong partnerships with colleagues, partners, government agencies and law enforcement, and most importantly, with the communities we serve."[19] They have a unit called Special Constables. "Their primary focus is engaging their communities in active crime prevention/reduction activities, and building positive relationships between their communities and the RCMP ... and they also have the capacity to provide tactical, enforcement and investigational support to other RCMP officers if required."[20] In addition, "these Community Constables have a valuable knowledge of the geography, culture and language in the communities they serve, and remain in those communities for the duration of their time as Community Constables."[21]

The RCMP has taken a wise and strategic approach to policing with the community. All our other police services across the nation are equally committed to this vision. It has great potential for healthier relationships, not only between the police and the community, but for all people to live in harmony. We trust that this vision to build bridges into the community ends up being more than just a nice principle, but a vision to be implemented and adhered to at operational levels. Indeed, the 'community constables' are well suited to serve in the communities because they are very familiar with the community

---

[18] www.rcmp-grc-gc-ca
[19] Ibid.
[20] Ibid.
[21] Ibid.

dynamics – landscape, culture, and language. This is what gives Tribal Police Services on First Nations Reserves an upper hand in community policing. True, this does not solve or eradicate all policing issues but it surely creates great potential for deeper and healthier relationships between the police and the community.

The Tribal Police Service on Wikwemikong Unceded Territory on Manitoulin Island, under the leadership of Chief Terry McCaffrey, has developed some strong collaborations with the residents. They operate from a well-informed perspective of understanding the community's needs, customs, and the rights of First Nations. The officers work with such strong cultural and traditional ties, and the philosophy of policing that emphasizes their well-known "7 Grandfather Teachings of: Love, Respect, Courage, Bravery, Honesty, Humility, and Truth."[22] One can imagine the environment created from having such shared core values.

Furthermore, given the First Nations' concepts of abiding by moral respect for all living creatures, each of the teachings are linked to an animal:[23]

1. Humility is represented by the wolf whose life is lived for his pack (as a sacred part of creation), and the ultimate shame for the wolf is to be outcast. The giving nature and devotion to protecting and working for the good of the wolf pack is a display of humility. The wolf acknowledges others - thinks about others before he thinks about himself. Therefore, think about how you impact the lives of others around you - you are part of pack.

2. Bravery (courage) is represented by the bear (the mother bear) whose courage and strength enables her to face her fears and challenges while protecting her young ones. This is about the courage to do the right thing.

---

[22] Wikwemikong Tribal Police Service has embraced the Teachings of the Seven Grandfathers, also known as the Seven Teaching or Seven Grandfathers, which is a set of teachings on human conduct towards others. These teachings from the elders are deeply respected among the Anishinaabe people and other First Nations around the country. Ojibwe.net

[23] Uniting Three Fires Against Violence: The Seven Grandfather Teachings. UT-FAV.org

3. Honesty is represented by the raven (the sabe) — being yourself and not someone we are not. This is about speaking from the heart. Historically, contracts and agreements were not written down on paper but were expressed in the shaking of hands - an expression of honesty.

4. Wisdom is represented by the beaver — using his natural gifts wisely for his survival. The beaver also alters his environment in an environmentally, friendly, and sustainable ways for the benefit of his family and his community. The beaver builds so that others will benefit from his use and application of wisdom.

5. Truth is represented by the turtle who carries the teachings of the earth on his back. He also lives a life of slow and meticulous manner since he understands the significance of both the journey and the destination. The turtle is also walking and leaving a trail for all to follow the great teachings of love, respect, courage, humility, wisdom, honesty, and truth.

6. Respect is represented by the buffalo who gives every part of his being to sustain the human way of living. He does this not because he is of less value, but because he respects the balance and needs of others. Respect is all about giving 'of yourself for others.'

7. Love is represented by the eagle who has the strength to carry all the teachings. He also has the ability to fly highest and closest to the creator and also has the sight to see all the ways of being from great distances. Since love is the core foundation of all the teachings, the eagle's feather is regarded as the highest honour and a sacred gift.

Indeed, First Nations have great insights for us to learn about how to relate to others in healthier ways. Our communities would have better relationships if we embraced and implemented these wise teachings.

Some Points to Ponder:

1. Police services could intentionally increase their visibility in the community through proactive approaches. Increased visibility contributes to crime prevention through the deterrent effect of police presence. Such attempts to increase police visibility in the community are enhanced through intentional collaborations with the community.

2. There would be wisdom in being deliberate in recruiting to ensure that the community's cultural diversity is reflected in the front-line officers, senior ranks, and support staff. Canada's history of early British and French immigrati/migration still has an effect on the overall composition of the police across in our nation. It seems a lot easier for their descendants to take on policing as a career, unlike those who have emigrated from places where communities and police forces have an adversarial relationship. These cultural and racial diversity matters must be taken seriously by any police service/jurisdiction desiring to serve the community effectively. One cannot ignore such matters and still hope to have healthier relationships with the community.

   A culturally diverse police service makes a powerful statement about policing with the community. It's far easier to build trust and friendship when communities within the community identify with officers. As with the case of police service boards, there should never be tokenism in recruiting culturally diverse officers; everyone must be recruited on the basis of set qualifications. Likewise, senior officers should also be sufficiently diverse so as to prevent the suspicion and negativity that can arise when the community sees a predominantly homogeneous top brass.

3. When patrolling or investigating, the police could provide some basic useful information to inform members of the public of what is going on. Generally, people become curious or suspicious when they see police officers

on the streets. Providing information in the course of interacting with people in the community helps to break communication barriers and facilitate the building of good rapport with members of the community. This can encourage citizens to collaborate with the police. Remember that when information is not voluntarily provided, people fill in the blanks on their own and often make uninformed conclusions on what they observe and believe is 'the truth'. This may undermine what would, otherwise, have been a productive interaction.

Of course, police officers routinely deal with classified and confidential information and operations and so it would not be wise to compromise an operation just to please the public. When police respond to a call, they act on information provided by dispatch, which is exclusively for police use. However, after having encountered a person appearing to fit a suspect's description and having assessed the situation, an officer's opening words could still provide ample information to invite collaboration.

For example, imagine pulling up into a shopping plaza and seeing several police cars in the front (obviously, something would have happened). You try to park in an empty space but a police officer steps up and says, "You can't park there. Please move your car," and so you do. However, a more collaborative mindset officer might approach the same situation in a different way: "You can't park there. There is an investigation going at the moment. Please move your car." Volunteering that little bit of information has great potential to create better and healthier relationships. In another scenario, for an officer to stop someone without providing any pertinent details may create and intensify tension, conflict, and confusion. Judiciously volunteered information may prevent potentially explosive situations.

4. The relationship between the chief of police and the Police Services Board is another key factor in the creation of

healthy working relationships for any police organization and the community. The police Executive Command Team would, in turn, reflect or resemble that relational dynamics. Developing such healthy and supportive relationships will contribute to better communities, regions, provinces, and country. The entire police organization is heavily influenced and shaped by the relationship between their commander and the Police Services Board. A deterioration of that relationship would, sadly, generally be acted out or displayed by the police officers in the course of carrying out their duties and responsibilities. Such approaches to acting out differences and relational wrinkles have negative impact. They have no benefit to the police service, the board, and the community. Healthier and more constructive alternative dispute and conflict resolution approaches should be employed to resolve issues.

Municipal police chiefs are appointed or elected officials entrusted with the responsibility of running the entire police organization. As one can imagine, this is not an easy task. Chiefs report directly to their Police Services Board, who themselves have a detailed job description for the chief and, on behalf of the community, monitor and evaluate the chief's performance according to the position's established goals and objectives.

Unlike municipal and regional police services, the Royal Canadian Mounted Police (RCMP) is organized under the authority of the *RCMP Act*, and is headed by the Commissioner who, under the direction of the Minister of Public Safety Canada, controls and manages the RCMP and all matters connected to their operations.

Provincial police organizations are accountable to civilian police commissions who conduct investigations into the police chiefs and officers when necessary. For example, in the event of incidents between the police and the public, or between police officers and individuals, the Special Investigation Unit (SIU) has investigative authority and can decide whether a criminal offence has taken place or not. Police enforce the law, but they are not above it. This is why the system enables citizens to file a complaint (via the Office of the

Independent Police Review Director in Ontario, for example) in cases where they feel police have wronged them. Such complaints are taken very seriously and are investigated.

The Association of Police Services Boards also governs police services through policy, hiring, and monitoring police performance as a commitment to fairness, equity, and adherence to the code of conduct, which includes:

1. Acting with honesty and integrity

2. Treating people with respect

3. Not abusing their powers and authority

4. Acting in a manner that does not discredit or undermine public confidence in the police service.

As we can see, these are not whimsical expectations. These are realistic, sustainable, and evaluable high standards. What this code of conduct does not tell us is that it is intricately connected to all other aspects of the police college curriculum. This curriculum is designed to train police officers to see and embrace a different world from what most people live in. As Dr. Kevin Gilmartin states quite frankly in his book, *Emotional Survival for Law Enforcement*, "From the first day of academy training, through an entire career of police work, officers have to learn to perceive the world as potentially hazardous in order to survive the streets."[24] Dr. Gilmartin calls this the world of "hypervigilance."[25]

Officers are trained to be extremely alert, with singular focus upon arriving at a call, reminding themselves that anything could happen, and that officer safety is a priority. For the most part, and rightly so, officers in these situations will inevitably relate to members of the public from within the context of hypervigilance. Evidently, with help from the media and personal experiences, some members of the community have contributed to these hypervigilance environments.

[24] Kevin Gilmartin. Emotional Survival for Law Enforcement: a Guide for Officers and Their Families. E-S Press, 2002, p.33.
[25] Ibid.

Thankfully, every call is different and requires its own appropriate response. The bottom line is that the community and police contribute to the creation of their shared environments, for better or for worse. This is why healthy collaborative efforts and intersections are needed. Such healthy working relationships emerge from intentional mutual collaborations. In consultation with each other through "learning conversations"[26] and perhaps facilitated by independent consultants, the police and the community might find value in reflecting on these questions:

1. What kind of a relationship do we want to have between us? *Define it.*

2. What do we want to see happen in our community? *Envision it.*

3. What does it take to see that happen? *Count the cost.*

4. What kind of culture needs to be created which will facilitate our goals and objectives? *Identify the ingredients.*

5. How do we ensure that this culture of intentional collaboration between the police and the community permeates and leaks through both parties?

6. How do we ensure that this culture permeates and leaks throughout the community?

7. What are the next steps toward our vision? *Think concrete next steps so that these ideas do not just end up in the basket of good intentions.*

---

[26] Douglas Stone, Bruce Patton, Sheila Heen. Difficult Conversations: How to Discuss What Matters Most. Penguin Books, 1999. All three authors are distinguished lecturers at Harvard University.

Chapter Eight
A Religio-Spiritual Perspective on Policing

The idea to include this chapter came to me one summer while attending a Sunday Worship Celebration at Harvest Bible Chapel in York Region, Ontario. The lead pastor, Reverend Paul Whittingstall, preached a sermon entitled "Life in the Public Square" (part of the series "Never the Same: The Gospel Changes Everything" based on Romans 13:1-7) about our relationship to the government. I was thrilled to hear a sermon along those lines, especially on something that related to what I was writing about. I was all ears when he started reading the Holy Scriptures (the Bible) that morning.

Basically, the gist of his presentation was:

1. We, as citizens and residents, must live in accordance with the government's unwavering commitment to treating all people fairly within the context of social justice and human rights.

2. Authorities are institutions placed by God's design

3. Authorities are God's servants

4. Governments have a job to do:

    a. Make laws for the good of human life

    b. Protect laws to ensure that people live in peace

5. Citizens likewise have a responsibility to fill:

    a. Be a community focused citizen - watch out for the needs of others (commit to treating everyone fairly)

    b. Pay your taxes and do not steal from the government

    c. Be people of integrity and do not cheat, cut corners, or be disrespectful

6. Where is the line to disobey the government?

    a. Be wise about what you choose to protest

    b. Do not break the law simply because you don't like the law

    c. You can stand up (within the law in Canada) against the government (and break the law), if the law violates human rights or supports expressions of dehumanizing or mistreating other people. The government must ensure the protection of the rights of all people at all times

    d. You can help in changing laws that do not uphold the value of life

7. Concluding remarks:

    a. The Gospel changes everything. It affects and influences our thought processes and behaviour

    b. In response to the Gospel, we must live above the world

    c. Your collaboration with the government must always be for the well being / welfare of all people. Government expressions of marginalizing or exploiting other people must be challenged by all responsible citizens

    d. Be an example to all people.

What a timely visit to the York Region Bible Harvest Chapel! What a delight it was to participate in a worship service where the leadership intentionally addressed the value of teaching worshippers their responsibilities to the government and the value of healthy relationships within the context of faith or religious liberty. Good job, Reverend Whittingstall!

Our Canadian government, like any other government in the world, is not perfect, as it is made up of human beings with feet of clay like the rest of us. We certainly have a good system, including human rights-based principles to serve and protect ourselves as a nation. We all have the privileged right to question or challenge those who subject us to unfair treatment. It is good to know that there are clearly established procedures that every citizen can use to have investigations and inquiries carried out by independent bodies.

As you can see, our behaviour is intricately connected to our various religious and cultural values. In most cultures around the world, there is recognition of the government as a representative of God or the divine. True, the government is made up of humans who are just as fallible as anyone else. In other words, it is possible for the government to make laws that do not uphold the intrinsic value of human life. Therefore, it would be safe to conclude that God is not responsible for the messes and tyrannical conditions created by some self-centred and egotistical governments in other parts of the world. Generally, the laws that are made by the government (of any country) should be designed for the good of all the people in that country. Therefore, the government, as God's representative, has the authority to rule and administer punishment on all violators of the law. This is where the police come in, as a representative of government in their respective communities and nations. Sadly, when there is no reverence for God within the government, self-serving laws will be insidiously drafted and introduced in parliament – be read, discussed, tabled, and get voted on (become law) and be enforced by the police, who are, basically, manipulated by shrewd members of the government for their personal gains. It is always sad to see the police being turned into puppets by unscrupulous leaders.

By the way, in Canada, the police represent the government and not a political party (or the ruling party). Sadly, policing is politically driven in some parts of the world, often making police officers expressions or representatives of the ruling party. One can only imagine how such politicized environments may create tremendous tensions and conflicts resulting in unhealthy and chaotic relationships. A politicized police organization finds itself in awkward and difficult situations, especially when there is a change in government or a new party in power. Indeed, there is wisdom in keeping the police as an organization separate from political parties. To know that the police are not politically manipulated helps to create ongoing stability in the nation and trust in the police jurisdiction.

The other point to bear in mind here is that police officers are themselves human beings and members of the community who happen to serve and protect their communities as representatives of the government. As government representatives, the police have the awesome responsibility to be honourable professionals who, through their words and deeds, deserve the trust and respect from their communities. Trust and respect are earned and learned virtues. There might be times when the public may not feel like respecting the police, possibly because of the impact of previous life experiences. This creates enormous tension between the police and the community, especially given the fact that police officers are representatives of the government. We can imagine the internal conflicts within police officers when their office and role as government representatives are disrespected by those whom they are charged to serve and protect. Such expressions of can have negative impact on the police officers. True, the level of professional integrity and ethical conduct displayed by police officers should not be inspired by the level of respect given by the public. Police officers are to have sincere dedication to their duty and responsibility of public service that is not conditional on disrespect or respect given by the public.

However, this is not a blind respect. Police officers have the awesome responsibility to execute their responsibilities with professionalism before expecting to receive respect. In other words, when police officers' behaviour or deeds leave a lot to be desired, it is difficult for the public to respect the police. This is a two-way street. Communities may creatively and collectively find ways to express honour, respect, and appreciation for their police, such as striking a small steering committee or planning events in consultation with the chief or commissioner of police. Invite the chief and other officers for a weekend event, perhaps, and use the community centre or school as a venue (which would be a neutral location to help with the power balancing). Create a short program, possibly including opening remarks, introductions of selected community representatives, words of greeting from the chief or commissioner, and a few minutes for clergy members to pray for officers. Have people line up to greet the chief or commissioner and have some finger foods at the end.

Prayer breakfast meetings aimed at praying for government leaders and agencies, as well as educational institutions in the community, can also build solidarity between the police and the community. The City of Markham's former mayor, the late Donald W. Cousens, left a legacy that will be remembered for many years to come. This Prayer Breakfast initiative is now an anticipated annual event drawing over 700 people to pray for government leaders, government representatives (including the police), and the people of the city. A simple hot buffet breakfast is served, followed by prayers for specific categories of individual positions in the community: government representatives, government agencies (police, fire fighters, and paramedics), directors of school boards, et cetera, and then followed by a keynote speaker. The primary focus is prayer, not the breakfast. Eric Tappenden, a seasoned influential community leader and business man, and a long-standing initial co-chair of the event, used to say toward the end of the breakfast, "We value your feedback on the prayer breakfast, but please do not waste your time commenting on the food. Our main focus is prayer." People chuckled each time he made that jocular but weighty remark. In fact, people received (and still receive) decent hot breakfasts every November since its inauguration. By the way, Eric is currently serving as co-chair of the York Regional Police Appreciation Night Committee. He is known in the community for his servant leadership, great respect and support for police officers.

The late Mayor Cousens' was a consultative and generational thinker, and his leadership style resulted from a rare synthesis of having been a Presbyterian minister and a politician. While the Markham Mayor's Prayer Breakfast is Christian based, it invites all of Markham's diverse denominations, religions, and faiths (including those of no faith). One time he was asked why he would initiate a Christian-based prayer gathering in the midst of such a plurality and diversity of religions. He replied, "I was convinced in my heart that there was need for a public gathering where people can pray in the name of Jesus Christ without apologizing to other faiths for not being politically correct. Other religions and faiths can also organize their own faith-based or no-faith gatherings, if they wish , and I would be delighted to attend and participate in such community focused gatherings."

Another unique feature of Markham's prayer gathering is the recognition and appreciation for all ministers, pastors, and religious leaders. Usually, they are all asked to stand as the audience is invited to give them a round of applause for their services in the community. A good number of those serving on the steering committee are also members of the clergy and come from diverse backgrounds. It really is a community building event.

This vision for the Mayor's Prayer Breakfast has spread to other neighbouring towns and communities (municipalities) across York Region, including Stouffville/Whitchurch, King City, Richmond Hill, and Newmarket. Indeed, this is an innovative way to facilitate the building of healthy relationships in the community, especially with government representatives. Another encouraging reality of this community event has been the tremendous financial support by local businesses. Several businesses support this event in various ways, including sponsoring high school students to attend this annual Prayer Breakfast. Such community events have great potential for far-reaching positive impacts on youth and the community as a whole It helps youth to value the essence of such a spiritual community-based gathering.

Some Observations and Considerations:

1. Canada is a culturally and religiously pluralistic country. Having a religion or no-religion is protected by law. In other words, each person has the freedom to believe or embrace any religion s/he wants without fear of being discriminated against.

2. One of the sad realities of our Canadian expression of pluralism is that some people view such diversity of religions and faiths, and their coexistence in society, as an opportunity to attempt to confirm that all religions are equal. Nothing could be farther from the truth because such an approach

to life would not be a realistic proposition. Attempting to unpack this point would be a subject matter for a separate book.

Suffice to say at this point, although all religions adhere to the golden rule of seeking to "treat others as you wish to be treated," we cannot, categorically, conclude that all religions are the same, because they are not. Although there are some renowned world leaders who have declared the sameness of all religions, that is a fallacy. That "sameness of all religions" assertion comes from a fallacious and ignorant standpoint. By virtue of their fundamental differences in origin, fundamental beliefs, practices, et cetera, all religions are mutually exclusive. One of the most eloquent thinker and voice on the exclusivity of religions is Ravi Zacharias, an East Indian born Canadian-American and the founder and Chair of the Board of Ravi Zacharias International Ministries. He has a few videos posted on YouTube and has written books and articles. Ravi highlights at least four distinct types of questions every religion attempts to answer: (1) with regards to origin of life/universe, (2) meaning or purpose of life, (3) morality (decisions about right and wrong), and (4) destiny (what happens after death). These points are worth noting.

3. As Canadians, we each have a moral and social obligation to stand up for each other's religious freedom. Therefore, if we witness or become aware that someone is being mistreated or discriminated against because of their religious beliefs, we should stand up for their rights, within the confines of the law, without reservation.

4. There is no Christian nation in the whole world. Yes, there are Christian or Judeo-Christian-based or influenced nations (including Canada), but they are not "Christian nations" because not *everyone* in those countries is Christian. The same would be true of other religions; there is no nation that can, categorically or truthfully, declare itself 100% one particular religion. True, the actions of the state, including all the laws and foreign relations decisions, may be wholly-based in that religion, so that even the beliefs and sentiments of the

non-practicing in the population have very little power or influence. Religion is really a matter of the heart and so it cannot be legislated for everyone. For example, Christianity is about having a personal relationship with God through Jesus Christ, and such a relationship with God cannot be legislated or mandated for everyone. Therefore, to hear anyone say, "We are a Christian country/nation," would be a misnomer. However, for someone to say that "we are a Christian-based/influenced country" would be closer to the truth, even though we may not all be abiding by those Christian (Judeo-Christian) principles.

5. There are faith-based fellowship groups (religious and social) within some police services. These groups meet regularly to provide practical expressions of spiritual, mental, emotional health and wellness among our police officers, and do so as peers. This is a commendable practice because life is holistic, and our officers need support in various aspects of life. It often takes just one person with a passion for something to get things organized by involving others in the process. Chaplains can also be a great resource in the strategic planning and execution of such ideas.

6. Remember, community efforts to organize public prayers or police appreciations by a place of worship leadership, in support of the police and their work, are generally well received. Just ensure that such efforts are initiated and organized in consultation with the chief's office, right from the beginning. Such initiatives have great potential for building and facilitating healthier relationships between the police and the community. We certainly hope that some of our churches, places of worship, and community groups will embrace these considerations and seek intentionally to bridge the gap between the police and the community and establish healthier relationships, as this is the primary objective of this book. Yes, it is possible for us to have good and healthier relationships between the police and the community. That will require hard work, intentionality, a clear vision, objectives, and a team-work mentality By the

way, YRP organizes 'a places of worship tour' for their new recruits as part of community outreach and building better relationships.

Chapter Nine
Deconstructing the Barriers:
Invitation to Partnership

While a commitment to eliminate all barriers between the police and the community may be unrealistic, it is still appropriate to work intentionally at breaking down those barriers. The goal is to eradicate these barriers through continued education. Therefore, within the spirit and context of realism, this chapter seeks to shed light on what could be done to facilitate better and healthier relationships between the police and their communities.

Chief Jolliffe's research, *Enhancing York Regional Police's Relationship with Its Visible Minority Communities* (March 2012), underscores the value and significance of proactive policing in the twenty-first century. Such an approach to policing requires intentional engagement in the community. Good, healthy, and collaborative relationships are key to effective policing.

Being collaborative in its nature and approach, community-based policing is the best philosophical and operational strategy for any police service today. As such, both the police and the community need to take deep and serious interest in understanding each other's fears, concerns, and interests. This does not come easily; it requires intentionally developing and heightening each party's inquisitiveness to gain mutual understanding that is deep enough to build high levels of trust. This extends beyond attending each other's events or gatherings, and beyond mere greetings, pleasantries, and casual interactions.

Trust is the key to healthier relationships. In his book, *The Speed of Trust – The One Thing That Changes Everything,* Stephen M.R. Covey is correct when he says:

> Trust impacts us 24/7, 365 days a year. It undergirds and affects the quality of every relationship, every communication, every work project, every business venture, and every effort in which we are engaged. It changes the quality of every present Moment and alters the trajectory and outcome of every future Moment of our lives—both personally and professionally.[27]

Furthermore, Covey provides us with the best and succinct definition of trust. He says:

> Simply put, trust means *confidence*. The opposite of trust—distrust—is *suspicion*. When you trust people, you have confidence in them—in their integrity and in their abilities. When you distrust people, you are suspicious of them—of their integrity, their agenda, their capabilities or their track record. It's that simple. We have all had experiences that validate the difference between relationships that are built on trust and those that are not.[28]

Indeed, trust is a priceless commodity that must not be compromised if a healthy working relationship is the goal. Of course, situations affecting mutual trust can and do arise. Trust is a fragile commodity that can be learned, earned, or lost. However, with progressive and creative effort, it can be rebuilt. It takes deliberate effort from all parties to create a favourable environment conducive to trust-building.

Among other factors, the process includes strategic efforts with measurable objectives endeavouring toward fruitful discussions, discoveries, and decisions for mutual benefit—but this is a two-way street. However, given the power imbalance factors, police services would be wise to initiate creative connections with the community.

[27] Covey, Stephen M.R. and Rebecca R. Merrill. The Speed of Trust: The One Thing That Changes Everything. Free Press 2006, p.1-2.
[28] Ibid., p.5

True, the onus is on the police to recognize this power imbalance and do something about changing our culture or behaviour. For an example, when a police officer in uniform walks by and and takes the initiative to acknowledge people and greets someone, "Good day/ Good evening," it enhances relationships and puts dignity in people. People respond a lot better to interactions that infuse dignity into them. By the same token, imagine what would happen if a police officer in full uniform were to pull over a car full of family members. The mother or father driving is spoken to in the presence of the family with disrespect or in dehumanizing ways. This would have a negative impact on the interaction dynamics and on the entire family, especially on their perception of the police. If there are children in the car, they will also learn and develop their opinion or perception about the police from that experience. In addition, how the adults will chose to process and talk about the experience in the presence of or with the children, impacts future interactions with the police.

In some cultures around the world, the man is regarded as the head of the home, and is always expected to be talked to with utter respect, especially in the presence of his family. Paying attention to such possible contexts will facilitate healthier relationships. A deep interest in someone does not just happen; it requires intentionality and is driven by a genuine care for people. Superintendent Veerappan is absolutely correct when he says, "Police officers need to constantly bring their humanity side first, before presenting their professional side." As representatives of the government, the police need to take ownership of the process while consultatively monitoring progress in partnership with the community itself. Such collaborative efforts may be complicated, challenging, and time consuming, but they represent measurable steps in the right direction on the part of the police. Results would most definitely be transformative in the community, nationwide, and globally.

Indeed, the police are people committed to serving the communities in which they also live. As representatives of government who ensure that laws of the land are upheld, police services represent the prevailing authority and power. As such, the onus is upon them to initiate efforts to strike a balance with the public, interacting with people from a position of care rather than one of force. For some, unfortunately, police presence has the propensity to deflate the confidence of even the best citizens in good standing. As you probably know, when people are nervous, they can exhibit questionable behaviour, thus catching the attention of our "hyper-vigilant"[29] police officers and possibly leading to unnecessary conflict. For those of us who have had negative or unhealthy experiences with police, it would take much more to develop the confidence necessary to interact normally with officers. Thankfully, this process of developing confidence and trust is not a mono-directional effort but a collaborative one.

Here are some practical suggestions (in no order of importance) on how to break down barriers to healthier relationships between police and the communities they serve:

1. **Police Week / Open House**: The police service could set aside at least one weekend per year to create opportunities at the police station, inviting the community to tour the building and learn about their services in the community. (York Regional Police service is a champion on these efforts to connect with the community). The police station Command Team would select specific dates, creatively and aggressively advertise a few months or so in advance, and noting the start and finish times; the chief or commissioner of police should be on site to greet members of the public; and flyers or pamphlets on the police and its services should be handed out to the public, with friendly officers on hand to help answer questions. Officers on hand would ideally be those most reflective of cultural and gender diversity. The team's composition has a subtle power to espouse or undermine efforts to improve community relations.

   The Shona people of Zimbabwe have a wise saying: *"Hukama igasva, hunozadziswa ne kudya,"* which literally means, "Friendships have gaps that are filled only by food." When people eat together, they generally relax, chat, and connect at deeper levels, and a good Police Week would be served well at the end by providing some finger foods representing the community's cultural composition.

---

[29] Kevin Gilmartin. Emotional Survival for Law Enforcement: a Guide for Officers and Their Families. E-S Press, 2002.

2. **Open House Attendance**: For their part, the community should accept the police's open house invitation en masse, as attending the event in good numbers would reflect support for the police. Of course, a well-attended Police Week also maximizes the event's potential to overcome relational barriers, diffuse tension, minimize misunderstandings, and overcome unhealthy fears.

3. **Crime Prevention Week**: It is said that education or awareness is the best protection against crime. This is an opportunity "to give people in the community the information needed to help themselves and others achieve the objective of creating safer and healthier communities."[30]

4. **Foot patrolling (for officers)**: The good old "walking the beat" approach is still relevant as it provides countless opportunities to interact with community members. Officers can observe things that are not otherwise visible from inside a police cruiser; deter criminal activity by "flying the colours;" create opportunities to engage in mutually insightful dialogue with members of the public; and greet or simply nod or acknowledge people as they make eye contact. Such opportunities are priceless when it comes to policing *with* the community to minimize barriers to healthier interpersonal communication.

5. **Foot patrolling (for the public)**: The sight and presence of police officers among them creates a sense of validation among law-abiding citizens, happy to know that their community matters enough that police will personally be on-site to serve and protect. When police officers greet or acknowledge members of the community, they show that they are human too and able to relate to people.

6. **Police officers in schools and post-secondary institutions**: Frequent on-site presence of police officers in our learning institutions shows a strong bond between police and members of the community. Such presence should be guided by the notion of 'policing with the school' rather than 'policing the

---

[30] www.oacp.on.ca>campaign

school.' The latter emanates from an authority base rather than an interest or friendship base. The difference is akin to that between getting the job done and being there as an ally who cares about the well-being of people in the community. Healthy relationships are crucial for effective policing.

It would be strongly indicative of an unhealthy relationship if community stakeholders were to protest police presence in learning institutions. Clearly, some unresolved conflict would have been allowed to fester and linger. Yet, if a law-breaking or violent incident were to take place in those learning institutions, the community expects the police to be first responders. Imagine the tension or impact of that conflict—to call the police (whom you protested against) to come and resolve the issues in the learning institution you had told them to stay away from. Let us not allow conflicts to deteriorate so far as to shut out the police from showing their colours frequently and patrol on our institutions of learning. True, frictions may arise, but there are solutions. Let us engage the services of independent conflict resolution practitioners who are skilled in interest-based solutions to have win-win results. Besides, we also want our young people to grow up into good and responsible community members who respect authorities and uphold the laws of the land. We can facilitate or undermine the creation of healthy relationships for our youth through our actions, words, and attitudes we display. Indeed, language and actions matter. "Deeds speak." We need to care about our children (young people) and their future, enough to teach them principles and values that support nation building and navigate the global community of diversity and inclusivity.

Remember our premise from previous chapters: Generally speaking, when there is a conflict between two parties, both parties would have contributed. We need to be humble enough to understand that despite our best intentions, the reality is that the things we do or say can be easily misunderstood by others. This can create tension, leading to conflict, and ultimately affect the relationship. This is why it is essential to maintain ongoing healthy dialogues between us.

Such disputes and conflicts could benefit from resolution efforts at town hall meetings designed to create opportunities for the parties to hear each other's perspectives and chaired by skilled interest-based conflict resolution practitioners.

7. **Social media:** Police services can capitalize on the use of computer-mediated technologies to facilitate the creation and sharing of information within communities. Obviously, a community's police service would identify opportunities on different social media platforms in accordance with policies and safety requirements for sharing information with the community.

Used constructively, social media can be a great tool for sharing and exchanging information promptly and leveraging efforts to build trust and mutual confidence between parties.

8. **Sports activities:** Organizing and participating in various sports events with members of the community can be an excellent way to build social bridges. Most police officers are committed to regular exercise, and so are many people in the community. There would be numerous opportunities for seasonal or regular sports between police and the community. Whether on the court, on the field, on the ice, or on the circuit, participating in sports activities with the goal of socializing provides police teams with opportunities to open new friendships and healthier relationships with the community.

9. **Volunteering:** In case you are not aware, York Regional Police officers are encouraged strongly to volunteer in some form of service in their community as part of their active duty. The goal is to engage the officers in finding opportunities to serve their communities as members of the community, who happen to be police officers. You can imagine the possible positive impact and dynamics created within such relational environments. By the way, not all police jurisdictions have such expectations for their officers, despite the fact that it's a great opportunity for officers to serve their communities from a different platform other than regular policing. Basically, they rub shoulders with

citizens, establish friendships along the way, and collaborate with other organizations through meeting the needs of real people in the community.

10. **Spring cleanup**: Communities in need of a cleanup present another opportunity for police and the community to team up for a good cause. Parks or littered roadsides can set the stage for a joint project like "Keep Our Streets & Parks Clean." Projects like these reward collaborative community-police projects with tangible, visible results, meeting real needs, and making a difference in the neighbourhood together.

11. **Getting to know our police officers**: Create opportunities for officers to share about their lives - life experiences as members of the community. This sharing could be done rotationally at neutrally perceived locations such as the community centre, the library, a school gym, or place of worship and it should feature various culturally diverse officers at a given time.

12. **Connecting with our youth**: Intentional efforts to connect and engage our youth ought to be a priority if we want to improve the relationship between the police and our young people. One of the best books written from the perspective of youth that sheds much light on and provides perceptive insights into the struggles to build better relationships within the context of the police and the community is *Both Sides of the Fence – Surviving the Trap* by Michael A. Amos. This is a must-read book for anyone interested in a real-life story about the real challenges being faced by young people in some of our neighbourhoods. Michael tells his life story from a candid and transparent perspective. Just the back-cover information is worth the salt of this book:

"The themes of Michael's story range from the psychological effects of being raised around violence to the mentality and decision-making process that develop in a child emerging from a low socio-economic status and a depressed physical environment.

In a tough and uncompromising style, Michael describes his journey from childhood and adolescence, when his mindset was shaped by an environment of gangs, guns, and drugs, to his finally questioning what was the truth, and how, over time and through many ups and downs, he was able to integrate into and become a productive member of Canadian society.

Having seen life from both sides of the fence, Michael A. Amos shares his story in the hope that it will make other young people from similar backgrounds understand some of the root causes of their situations and realize that there is another side and there are other possibilities. It is also Michael's hope that *Both Sides of the Fence* may serve as a catalyst for change by providing law enforcement officers, social services, government agencies, and the general Canadian population with insight into the causes of the destructive behaviour of these young people."[31]

Indeed, there is great need to invest in building healthier working relationships between our young people and the police. Remember, the youth are not just the leaders of tomorrow, but also of today. Failure to lay relationally solid foundations for better relationships leads to dysfunctional dynamics today and tomorrow. However, all these attempts must be initiated in consultation with the youth themselves. As someone once said, "Whatever you do for me without me, is not for me." These young people are very creative, and partnering with them in these initiatives would result in tremendous possibilities and nuances of establishing and cementing better working relationships.

Obviously, this is not an exhaustive list of suggestions on possible creative ways and means of opening new doors to a healthy working relationship within the community. As both parties engage in "learning conversations"[32] more suggestions would emerge and be evaluated before they can be integrated into a strategic plan. Again, the first step

[31] Michael A. Amos. Both Sides of the Fence – Surviving the Trap. Famos Books, 2014. Permission to use this quote was granted by the author.
[32] Douglas Stone, Bruce Patton, and Sheila Heen, Difficult Conversations: How to Discuss What Matters Most, The Harvard Negotiation Project 1999.

toward healthy and friendly working relationships is the willingness to engage in open dialogue that informs decisions on how to collaborate toward a relationally healthier community. There has to be a shift from *monologue* to *dialogue*, and active listening to each other. This preferred shift or process needs to intentionally include our youth if we desire to introduce and retain long lasting effect for the generations to come.

Chapter Ten
The Take Aways

The bottom line is, the path to healthier relationships between the community and the police is an invitation to journey together. It does not happen overnight. Indeed, healthy relationships are key to effective policing and safe communities. In other words, effective policing involves community engagement (healthy interactions with members of the community), facilitates crime prevention, and that results in safer communities. When the police and the community have established healthy relationships, all expressions or forms of dysfunctions would be dealt with collaboratively and without strife or expressions of animosity because there would be caring spirit between them. Such relationally healthy environments also make it difficult for criminals to survive and function freely in the community.

Being in position of power, the police have the awesome and complicated task of initiating such preferred relationships through intentional collaborative community initiatives and educational efforts, and creatively inviting the community into "learning conversations."[33] Both parties, the police and the community, would have to work hard together to experience such healthy relationships. We need to intentionally create opportunities for dialogue. Bear in mind that, sharing the impact of our life experiences within safe contexts of 'learning conversations,' shape our identity, feelings, and truth telling in hugantic ways. Creating such safe contexts require curiosity, intentionality, work, humility, mutual respect, and skill.

---

[33] Douglas Stone, Bruce Patton, Sheila Heen. Difficult Conversations: How to Discuss What Matters Most. Penguin Books, 1999. All three authors are distinguished lecturers at Harvard University.

Some key take aways highlighted in this book are:

1. Police officers who are physically, socially, emotionally, mentally, and spiritually healthy, provide excellent public service.

2. Effective policing is a by-product of community engagement and policing with the community.

3. Intentional partnership between the police and the community is indispensable for creating safer and relationally healthier communities.

4. Dispute and conflict resolution, negotiation and mediation are key integral aspects of regular frontline policing.

5. Police officers who are friendly and equipped with alternative dispute and conflict resolution, negotiation and mediation skills contribute positively to effective policing in our communities.

6. Generally speaking, when there is a conflict between the Police and the Community, both sides have contributed to that conflict.

7. The police and the community can collaboratively create a new culture for mutual benefit.

8. Due to the power imbalance reality, the police should take the initiative to engage the community toward a healthier relationship.

9. Healthier relationships are all about healthy interactions.

10. Healthy interactions are all about listening to each other.

11. Listening to each other is all about being human.

12. Being human is all about friendliness.

13. Friendliness is all about caring for others.

14. Caring for others emerges from compassion, which facilitates collaboration.

15. Collaboration creates safer and relationally healthier communities.

The absence of healthy relationships create hordes of dysfunctions in life (homes, workplaces, schools, streets, and between the police and the community). People do not have to be the best of friends or agree on everything in order to work together, but they can be friendly with each other in their interactions. It seems that all cultures worldwide value friendliness, though we know that not all people are friendly. Indeed, becoming friends requires collaboration.

Police officers who are friendly will naturally seek to resolve community issues through interest-based resolution approaches. Their interest-based alternative dispute and conflict resolution skills will always emerge and enhance effective policing, wherever they are. These are special police (peace) officers who:

1. Value people. They care deeply about the people they serve.

2. Value relationships. They care about healthy interactions with others.

3. Value learning (education). They care about discovering information and options.

4. Value diversity. They care about being inclusive in outlook and in practice.

5. Value skills. They care about becoming better at bringing peaceful solutions to situations using their professionally acquired skills.

6. Value friendships. They care about being friendly; perceiving people as potential friends, seeking to make each interaction start and end on a friendly note. Yes, friends may misunderstand each other, disagree, and even have conflicts. Even in those situations, those in highly valued friendships have a disposition to find ways to resolve differences amicably. Every now and then I hear stories or comments from people who say, "One time, I was pulled over by the

police because I was speeding. The officer was one of the friendliest cop I've ever met—very nice, respectful, and professional. Although I got a speeding ticket, I was not upset by that because the interaction I had with the police officer was pleasant." Such stories bring a thrill to my heart. Imagine the impact of sharing such positive life experiences within our network of friendships.

Such friendly dispositions are indicative of healthy relationships in other contexts of police officers' life. Healthy relationships are irresistibly infectious. In other words, the friendships established, cultivated, and maintained with the supervisor and within the platoon (including the parade briefings and pep talks) have direct influence on team performance. What an officer does on-duty or off-duty impacts others. The days of lone-ranger police officers are long gone. Effective policing is a team effort, and each officer must collaborate with colleagues as teammates, and with the public.

Furthermore, we must not overlook the perspectives of the police about the public. Given the nature of what police officers do, day in and day out, sometimes they see the best as well as the worst side of human behaviour. For example, officers see the caring and acts of kindness people give to each other (including strangers). The flip side is that they also witness horrendous acts of violence, brutality, hatred, discrimination, and the like. They also celebrate with their communities, in the low times and in high times. Indeed, police officers live constantly with mixed feelings.

Their work is unpredictable, especially for front-line officers. A response to a call or a regular traffic stop can turn into some surprise or discovery that can transform their lives instantly and forever, turning that incident into a good or a bad experience. Sometimes they are fortunate to approach a given situation with some background information, and other times, facts simply unfold before their eyes as they carry out their duties and responsibilities.

Such environments, especially the bad experiences, take a toll on the officers emotionally, intellectually, physically, socially, and spiritually.

That is the reason for this "hypervigilance."[34] The biological processes officers undergo while on duty heighten their awareness, thinking abilities, and quick response to anything that comes up, according to Dr. Kevin Gilmartin.

A police 'officer's worldview' provides perspectives on the community and the individuals within it. There are at least four such perspectives emanating from the "officer's worldview," including:

1. That perspective which is acquired through the police college/academy. Officers are trained to look at people and at situations through certain lenses:

   a. Human rights

   b. The nature of the call they are on

   c. The procedures in place for such a situation

   d. Guidelines/regulations to be employed for that situation

   e. Limits of the law in that situation

   f. Professionalism and ethics

   g. Accessibility for people with disability

   h. Mission, vision, and core values of the police service

2. That perspective which is acquired through interaction with their colleagues. Officers discuss situations and compare notes.

3. That perspective which is acquired or informed by the media. The media has tremendous influence on how officers perceive themselves and their world.

4. That perspective which is acquired through personal experiences. From their regular responses to different calls and interacting with citizens, experience has taught them

---

[34] Kevin Gilmartin. Emotional Survival for Law Enforcement: a Guide for Officers and Their Families. E-S Press, 2002.

some important lessons, which are etched in their conscious and subconscious minds. Yes, they are aware that there are some people who like them, and others who dislike them. Unfortunately, often the negative encounters outweigh the positive ones, and ultimately contribute to an officer expecting the worst to occur in most incidents. Hypervigilance sets in as soon as they put on their uniforms and attach their equipment.

Indeed, the police uniform, the police car, the bike, and all the other equipment provide police officers with a tool kit and subsequently contribute to the tool kit mindset. That mindset requires regular balanced voluntary objective adjustments in accordance with the situation at hand, while bearing in mind that the tool kit is really designed to maintain peace. Police officers, strictly speaking, are *peace officers*—peace makers, peace keepers, and peace builders. To see and understand all police equipment from the perspective of maintaining peace should revolutionize officers' use of force. This calls for tremendous balance in every aspect of their lives.

The late Mr. L.E. Maxwell, Founder of Prairie College (Three Hills, Alberta) once said, "One of the hardest things to do in life is to maintain healthy balances." There is a lot of truth in this statement. This book tries to balance perspectives of the police and of the public in an attempt to draw them together so that both parties may create opportunities for learning conversations, resulting in healthier working relationships in our communities, towns, cities, and right across the nation.

The invitation is to both the police and the community to create opportunities for open dialogues (both formal and informal) and engage in true learning opportunities so that both parties can map out a better future together. Healthy relationships do not just happen. They emerge out of formal and informal interactions, and from creating opportunities to do things together within contexts of mutual trust and respect. Our mindsets and behaviours are intricately linked to our environments, biases, beliefs, and culture which may create relational barriers. Therefore, it is very important that we create opportunities that will give us new experiences to explore the barriers cause factors and our conclusions. As we acknowledge, assess, and measure the impact of our experiences on ourselves, begin to see the need to adjust our mindsets and behaviours.

Some Points to Ponder:

For the police:

1. Bear in mind that you were (and still are) a member of the community before you answered the call to be a police officer. You were not born a police officer. Please relate to all people as a caring member of the community When you use your position and title to amplify your humanity, you allow your uniform to become a conduit to your humanity - displaying the highest quality expressions of respect, compassion, and human rights in your public service.

2. Exegete your communities through learning their formal and informal (street) languages and cultures so that you can relate to them at extraordinary levels and build healthier relationships.

3. Community-focused police services with culturally diverse and gender inclusive civilians on their governing boards increase the community's trust in the police.

4. Sharing key roles (among police and civilian experts) builds community trust. For example when the police hires and engages highly skilled and highly qualified civilians to carry out some tasks within the police jurisdiction (performance reviews, conflict management systems, workplace fairness analysis, staff/employee grievances, et cetera), the community feels included in 'the policing with the community.' That adds numerous brownie points into the relationship.

5. Creatively increasing accountability to the public helps to build public trust, like organizing regular town hall meetings at a school or community centre to provide relevant information to the community.

6. Creating safe channels and opportunities for frontline police officers to share with their supervisors or the executive command team about policing impact on their life and work experiences (with regards to personal matters or views, organizational, judicial, and community issues).

7. Police promotions and performance reviews could also include their relational skills, peer reviews, and how officers connect with the community and not solely on policing skills, statistics generated from regular reports, and evaluations by supervisors. There would be wisdom in using the 360-degree feedback approaches because of the holistic nature of policing.

8. Develop a mindset that seeks to capitalize on opportunities to connect with the community. The York Regional Police officer who rapped at a Strada car show is an excellent example of police capitalizing on opportunities to outreach. That impromptu freestyle was priceless PR for the police (Google: *yrp officer rapping*). Listen to the positive comments from the organizer and see how the crowd responded enthusiastically to the song.

9. Trust and respect are two-way streets that emerge from professionalism. They flow better when they are reciprocated. It is difficult to earn trust and respect from the community when the community does not sense or feel trusted and respected. When the police display trust and respect in the community, public confidence in the police will increase proportionately. Remember, respect, according to First Nations "Teachings of the 7 Grandfathers," is a selfless characteristic - all about 'giving to others' as represented by the buffalo who supplies food to people with everything he has.

10. The relationship between the police and government should always be healthy, collaborative, and transparent. In other words, it is healthy and wise for the government to intentionally dialogue with the Association of Chiefs of Police prior to seeking to introduce laws that impact

policing. Failure to dialogue contributes to unnecessary tension between the government and the police, and then the police has to play catch up to enforce the laws.

11. The police, as government representatives, demonstrate the government's values (not the values of the ruling party).

12. The police uniform does not define who you are. In fact, you define the uniform by representing good governance and core values: respect and dignity for all people, professionalism, courtesy, friendliness, love, courage, honesty, wisdom, humility, truth and proper use of authority. How the police carry out their duties and responsibilities should help people connect the dots in their lives and have faith in the government and the police. In other words, the presence of police officers should create a sense of safety, protection, and tranquility in people. Unhealthy relationships are characterised by suspicion and unhealthy fear.

13. Your office and position as police officers should enhance your service to the community and the profile and legitimacy of policing in the eyes of the public.

14. As you rub shoulders with people in the course of carrying out your duties and responsibilities, be intentional about capitalizing on opportunities to build bridges that facilitate mutual trust and respect. Develop people skills that help the public to see you as a real person – friendly and professional, with a heart to connect with and serve people by:

    a. Being approachable …

    b. Acknowledging people's presence …

    c. Recognizing and acknowledging people's emotions …

    d. Displaying welcoming body language …

    e. Smiling and nodding at people …

    f. Maintaining eye contact in your conversations …

g. Being sensitive to the situation at hand …

h. Practicing listening skills …

i. Talking to people respectfully …

j. Asking sincere questions …

k. Applying de-escalation techniques (alternative dispute and conflict resolution skills) as a way of life …

For the Community:

1. Police officers are, first and foremost, human beings like all of us. They are members of the community who happen to serve as police officers. They were members of the community before they got hired, as police officers and they continue to be members of the community after they were hired. They have perceptions, emotions, identity, egos, and limitations, like all of us. They also have need for a sense of acceptance, sense of worth or significance, et cetera. Let us facilitate healthy relationships with them in the light of these common realties that join us as human beings.

2. Trust and respect for the police is reciprocal. The police earn trust and respect by giving the same to people in the community. Let us also do our part of giving respect to police officers as they carry out their duties and responsibilities.

3. For the most part, we all act out of our past experiences and acquired information. Let us revisit our past in order to rebuild new relationships with the police without allowing the past to rob us of new opportunities before us to build healthier relationships today.

4. We have tonnes of information available at our finger tips today, and some of it may be twisted or exaggerated depending on the motive of the author or communicator. True, some police officers have, regrettably, smudged the reputation of the police in the community. However, the majority of police officers are men and women of virtue

who are 100% committed to serving and protecting their communities. As Sergeant Adamson says, "Beware of media frenzy—feeding the public with only one view of things."

The police need the assistance of the community in order to be effective, "The police are the public, and the public are the police."[35]

5. Absorb yourself into a culture of people who help you to build healthier relationships in society, especially with the police. As Rev. Bryan Swash says, "If you engage with those who feed on distrust, you will start to think like them." Therefore, be a change agent who helps others to be better citizens and residents in the community.

6. There is a fundamental collapse of trust and a disrespect for authority in society today. Let us be intentional in our communities about guiding and mentoring others, especially our youth, to respect authority figures like their elders, parents, teachers, as well as police. If we do not help our young people to embrace and value respect for authority, we are setting them up for dysfunctional relationships. However, this collapse of trust and respect can be revived on condition that symbols of authority (including the police) demonstrate journeying toward:

   a. Alignment with human rights

   b. Respect

   c. Trust

   d. Professionalism

   e. Competence

   f. Accountability

   g. Holistic and inclusive core values

[35] Robert Peel. Quotes@BrainyQuote.com/quotes/robert_peel_260231 (1800's)

7. Be open to seeking to build new relationships with the police and to creating learning conversations for better and healthier outcomes.

8. Be willing to accept invitations to participate in either educational or informational opportunities to get to know the police in your community (open house, police week, crime prevention sessions, et cetera).

9. As you know, volunteerism is the backbone of Canadian life. Consider connecting with your local police service to find out what type of volunteer opportunities might appeal to you. Usually, there are many possible opportunities for all ages, depending on your passion and skill sets. Volunteering with the police provides members of the community with insightful opportunities to get to know the police in some special ways while serving their communities.

For Both - the Community and the Police

Life being so daily, there are some very difficult and complex situations that arise or happen in life. Sometimes, there are no easy solutions to some of life's situations. Consequently, it becomes very difficult to revisit, discuss, unpack, or analyze those situations. Without going into the complex details of the subsequent circumstance of what really happened …

1. How does a family or friend of someone shot and killed by the police relate to the police, let alone relate to the officer who fired the fatal shot?

   a. Is there value in bringing the two parties together to engage in some healing process?

   b. What assistance could be made available to the families and friends?

2. How does a family or friend of a police officer relate to the member of the community who killed the officer in the line of duty?

3. Hurt and pain are very real. Failure to deal with them constructively can lead to serious relational dysfunctions or catastrophic outcomes. How do these families and friends (police and community) cope with such real hurt/pain issues of life?

4. How does a police service create and maintain enough trust within the community to ensure that witnesses to crimes come forward and collaborate with the police in identifying perpetrators of crimes and violence without putting their lives in danger? Bear in mind that these witnesses may live in rough neighbourhoods with the fear of being labelled sellouts or snitches.

5. How does the community develop trust in the police it perceives negatively with regards to treatment of certain races or people groups? When a people group in the community "perceives" or "feels" that they are unfairly targeted by the police, what would it take to adjust or change such a "reality"? What resources are available to navigate that process? Perceptions and feelings are "real"/realities based on experiential knowledge.

6. How do the police respond to a call for help or an emergency in environments they are not welcomed, or have been told to stay out of? Such contexts must take mental and emotional tolls on the officers responding to the calls. How does one embrace professionalism, a positive attitude, friendliness, and humanity within such environments?

7. Considering that police training is specialized and all-encompassing—intellectually, emotionally, physically—the training requires ongoing updates and revisions to ensure that the police culture deals with root problems relating to policing in the twenty-first century using modern tools. For example, as it was the case in some parts of the United States of America when black people began to revolt against their mistreatment and sought their liberation from slavery, they were perceived as threats who needed to be subdued and dealt with ruthlessly. Consequently, the "the patrollers –

men on horsebacks, was all about hunting down run–away slaves."[36] These 'patrollers' (policemen) were created to police, capture, subdue, and beat up slaves into obeying them and their masters. Since the present is strongly linked to the past, that dark history of the United States of America, has ongoing implications on the relationship between the police and African Americans today. In other words, sadly, it is quite possible for a police department (service) to maintain and perpetuate a mindset, consciously or unconsciously, that would approach, differently, certain people groups in the communities where they serve. Such environments would create heightened tensions, frustrations, distrust, dislike, hatred, and conflicts between the police and those people groups.

Therefore, police services would be wise to have intentional training that provides well-rounded and holistic relational tools to equip their officers to be agents of social change. They must be made aware of the value of cultural diversity and inclusion in effective policing within the community today. Furthermore, the trainers of these officers would need to be transformational leaders with cultural awareness, the ability to objectively critique their biases, have intercultural dynamics, educational acumen, relational skills, diversity, and experiential knowledge to effectively train at such levels. What kind of resources are available to ensure such inter-cultural values and realities are incorporated in police officer training?

8. Considering that our youth are the leaders of today and tomorrow, investing in their education and learning to co-exist in this inter-culturally global village would have far-reaching positive outcomes for the betterment of life globally. How can the community and the police team up to bring awareness of the intrinsic value of cultural diversity and inclusion, co-existence, and empowerment in supporting the youth to flesh this out in real life? How do

[36] George Sullivan, Harriet Tubman - In Their Own Words, 2001, p.21

we effectively impart such values in our youth? What resources are we willing to set aside and invest in them? Are we prepared to pay the price for a better future?

The bottom line is that collaboration between the police and the community is necessary for effective policing and establishing a healthier working relationship between the two. Besides, the police needs the community, and the community needs the police. Remember, "The police are the public, and the public are the police."[37] Let us work together to make our communities and our nation the envy of the world!

True, there is a price tag attached to that reality. The question is, are we collectively ready to pay the price, get our hands dirty, and engage in learning conversations? Can we *dialogue, discover, and decide* on a way forward? Let all of us who share this land show our appreciation for each other by collaborating in our communities and contributing to healthier working relationships while being grateful to the indigenous peoples who welcomed us here.

Remember, whenever there is a conflict between people, both parties have contributed. Let us, therefore, be humble enough to identify our own contributions to any dysfunction and collaboratively chart a new direction for the future. It's never too late to start doing the right things.

Healthy working relationships between the police and community contribute to healthier and safer neighbourhoods, and that should be the desire of every responsible member of any community. You see, every time we hear about the police and the community at loggerheads, it should drive us to pressure community leaders to prioritize alternative dispute and conflict resolution. Our police and their governing boards are ultimately accountable to the people they serve. Considering all that specialized training they receive for the purposes of serving and protecting the people, the police ought to be held accountable for how

[37] Robert Peel. Quotes@BrainyQuote.com/quotes/robert_peel_260231 (1800's)

they carry out their duties and responsibilities. In other words, police behaviour and actions ought to display the excellence of their training. This explains why citizens have a lot of say on how the police and governing boards operate. Of course, citizens also have a responsibility, and would be wise to dialogue collaboratively with the police toward mutually agreed collective goals and objectives. We need each other, even though sometimes we needle each other. Therefore, let us get to know each other better so that we can work together better!

Indeed, the path to healthier relationships and true partnership is intentional, sacrificial, mutually beneficial, and all encompassing. The wise words of Lilla Watson, the Australian Indigenous visual artist, take 'partnership' to a higher level when she says, "If you have come here to help me, you are wasting your time. But if you have come because your liberation is bound up with mine, then let us work together."[38] Although this quotation is crafted and articulated within a context of political and economic liberation, we can rightly apply it in this context of seeking to build healthier relationships in our communities because we are intricately connected to each other as human being. Remember, there is only one race: the human race. Accordingly, we are being encouraged to view our partnership and coexistence as inseparable, and rightly so, because "the public are the police, and the police are the public."[39]

In keeping with the title of this book, *Community Policing: The Path to Healthier Relationships*, the concept of The Path is loaded with meaning and various nuances:

1. It is not "a Path" but "the Path" which is distinct from other paths.

2. It requires work to create a path.

3. Who pays for the creation of this path?

4. Who creates or designs the vision (the game plan) for the path?

5. Who evaluates the plan?

---

[38] Lilla Watson, Our Liberty is Bound Together: Invisible Children.com
[39] Robert Peel. Quotes@BrainyQuote.com/quotes/robert_peel_260231 (1800's)

6. Whose blueprint will be followed in creating this path?

7. Who are the key players (stakeholders) in the creation or planning process?

8. What qualifies that plan to be selected and implemented?

9. Who is going to invest in what is needed in the planning process?

10. Someone must trail blaze that path. Who will do that?

11. There ought to be a reason, an objective, or desired outcome for creating that path.

12. Where does the path lead to?

13. Is this path private or public?

14. If the path is public, as this one is, are there signs or markings along the way to help people follow?

15. Do the signs need to be explained or updated?

16. Is this path well known in the community?

17. Do you travel on this path alone or you need to be with others?

18. Do we need guides on this path?

19. If yes, who identifies and selects the guides?

20. How transparent is the selection process?

21. Who maintains this path?

22. Whoever maintains the path, to who do they report?

23. What is the criteria for evaluating and ensuring that things are going well?

24. How is the report submitted?

25. How often will the report be made?

26. What can be expected along the path?

27. Should there be rules and regulations for the path?

28. Who sets the rules and regulations for the path?

29. What is the criteria for those drafting the rules and regulations?

30. What happens to those who choose not to follow the rules and regulations set for the path?

As you can see, there are many intricate aspects to the notion of "The Path" that need special attention. The points above are not exhaustive. Most likely, you would be able to add a few more of your own.

Therefore, let us—the community and the police—enter into this Path of working and walking together toward healthier and thriving relationships that facilitate the creation of safer communities. Together, we can establish relationally healthier communities through intentional collaboration!

Therefore, let us …

☞ **Dialogue** openly to learn about each other

☞ **Discover** information about each other

☞ **Decide** on the next steps together

Let us work together!!!

Niigon Abin Resolutions Services

We are an independent consultancy specializing in:

• Conflict Management Systems ...

- alternative dispute and conflict   resolution

- mediation and negotiation

- workplace fairness assessments (analysis)

- workplace justice restorations

- creating a conflict resolution culture

- enhancing healthier working relationships

- emotional, mental, & spiritual intelligence (wellness)

• Life Coaching

• Workshops, Seminars, Conference speaking

• Youth Mentorship Opportunities

Our work includes police services/jurisdictions, children/youth & family services, community organizations, families, schools, colleges/ universities, workplaces, and places of worship (boards, members).

Remember, unresolved conflicts are very Costly!!!

Connect with Niigon Abin Resolutions Services

☞   To arrange for a speaker

☞   To arrange for customized training

☞   To order books

☞   Email: dr.mpindu@niigonabin.com

☞   Visit: www.niigonabin.com

Acknowledgements

Countless individuals have participated in the production of this book. There is a raft of special friends to whom I would like to express my heartfelt appreciation and special gratitude. Without their support, this book would not have been written. I am grateful for their support and feel deeply humbled that through their input and insights, the inspiration to write this book evolved. I am very much aware that I do not live in a bubble of 'me, myself, and I.' My life is intricately linked to those around and before me, and that my life's activities, accomplishments, and responsibilities are extensions of my interactions with others— face to face dialogues, readings, observations, and hearing stories from within the community and within police environments.

The Police and the Community

By virtue of my constant dialogues within these two contexts, my worldview has been shaped in remarkable ways. The names highlighted below may not mean much to you, but to me, they are priceless. They form part of 'my diary' of individuals who have contributed to my betterment as a global citizen. I do not have ample space to include everyone in this book project.

Special thanks are extended to:

Police Related Friends:

- Retired Chief of York Regional Police (YRP), Mr. Armand LaBarge, for presenting me with a life-changing opportunity to join and serve the YRP family as a chaplain. This enriching experience has, in special ways, catapulted me to the start of a new journey. You are a courageous and collaborative leader. We are aware that sometimes you made changes that were deemed unpopular at the time, yet good for the future of the organization. Thank you, sir.

- Retired Chief Eric Jolliffe (YRP), for your support and encouragement. I find your signature salutation refreshing when you ask me, "How are you doing, my friend?" Your inclusive leadership style, along with your devotion to healthy relationships, makes you a unique and effective leader. It was your MA thesis in Leadership at Royal Roads University that opened me up to such a great wealth of information and special insights into your perceptive, transformational, and relational leadership style. Thank you sir.

- Chief Jim MacSween (YRP) - you are a community focused transformational leader with excellent people skills. Thank you for your encouragement and expressions of support.

- Commissioner Thomas (Tom) Carrique, Ontario Provincial Police (OPP), you are an innovative transformational leader who highly values professionalism and people.

- Mr. Bruce Herridge, former Director of Ontario Police College (OPC), I wish you knew how much you inspired me, periodically, to keep sharpening my distinctive value (DV). Your leadership and operational skills are inspirational.

- Chief Wayne Kalinski, Orangeville Police service (OPS), you are insightful, an encourager, and a good friend indeed.

- Chief Paul Pedersen, Sudbury Police service (SPS), you are a down-to-earth transformational leader who is dedicated to policing with the community.

- Chief Jean-Michel Blais (retired), Halifax Regional Police (HRP), you contributed remarkably to making HRP a good example of a multiculturally diverse police service in our nation. Thank you for your servant leadership.

- Chief Stephen (Steve) Tanner, Halton Regional Police Service, you are committed to putting humanity (Ubuntu) behind the police badge. Thank you for 'acknowledging other people' in the path of life.

- Superintendent Ricky Veerappan of the Diversity, Equity, and Inclusion Unit (YRP), for your insights as I wrote this book. You were such a breath of fresh air whenever we met to compare notes I learned a lot more about policing from you, and you also allowed me to learn a lot about you as a member of the community who happens to be a police officer. Thank you for allowing me to bounce some of my ideas off you along the way. It is good to have you on the team.

- Inspector Gary Miner (retired), for being a true friend indeed in assisting and encouraging me to remain objective during my season of cognitive and emotional fog.

- My other YRP friends: Deputy Chiefs André Crawford, Robertson Rouse, and Brian Bigras; Superintendents Heidi Schellhorn, Stuart Betts, Alvaro Almeida, Stan Coley (retired), Tony Cusimano (retired), Keith Merith (retired), and Mark Brown (retired), Douglas Conley, Karen Noakes (retired), Carolyn Bishop (retired), Graham Beverly, Chris Bullen; Inspectors Shelley Rogers; Staff Sergeants Alice Tsang, Stu Gamer, Paul Chiang, Doug Bedford, Ed Burke, Joan Randall (retired), John Scheldon (retired); Sergeant Dave Track (retired); James D. Provis, Detective Pat Giberson (retired); Dr. Kyle Handley, Dr. Gary Marshall - for your professional support and encouragement; Police Constables – Detective Stephen Morrell – you are a servant leader, Pete Nyagie, Stephanie Postill-Hunter, Nigel Cole, Amaree Watkis, Jeremy Brewster, Trevor Burke, Lynne Connery, David Chen, Kambiz Nadoushan, Rebecca Roach, Malcolm Macdonald, Babak Hashemi, Chris Price, Dexter Jarad, Rey Corpuz, Nik Yun, Imtiz Manjra, Patrick Brown, Eon Lam, Sam Azzouggagh, Liana Storoniak, Carl Jeddes, Douglas James (a servant leader – brushing off snow from a senior's car), Matt Robins, Mark Hilliker, Karen Chen, Amjed Kaan, Jason Griffiths, Kwame Agyei, Reuben Thompson, Detective Paul Marisette, Elvis Lee, Eric Tang, Tommy Kim, Ashleigh White, Colin Alexander, Matthew Ma, Warren Owen, J. Wayne Young, Eric Tam, Pavol Zec, Victoria Masson, Jeff David Vandenbos, Andre Boteju, Dana Cuff, Rebecca Reznicki, Elvis Lee, Jeff Bailey, and Santosh

Choubey; Auxiliary Selma D'Souza; Winnie Wales (Administrative Assistant) retired; and all the police officers I have gone with on rides-along in the cruiser. I do not have ample space to highlight all your contributions. I am a better citizen because of your friendship. As someone has rightly concluded, "Show me your friends, and I can tell your future You are my good friends in this path toward healthier relationships."

- My colleagues/fellow YRP chaplains: Rev. Canon Greg Symmes (retired), Rabbi Mendel Kaplan, Rev. Vicki Cousins, Pastor Dr. Mansfield Edwards, Father Damian Young-Sam-You, Imam Abdul Hai Patel, Herbie Kuhn, The Rev'd G.E. Bailey – your friendship and support has meant a lot to me over the years. I also appreciate the contributions of the three chaplains who are no longer part of the current "God Squad," Father John Borean, Rev. Dr. Bill Thornton, and Rev. Mavis Fung. Thank you.

- My other chaplain friends: Rev. Dr. Jeremiah Doyce, Chaplain General of Zimbabwe Republic Police (ZRP), Superintendent Rev. Vulindela Jamela, Provincial Chaplain (ZRP), Masvingo, Rev'd. Fr. Stephen E.R. Davies, The Royal Bahamas Police Force (RBPF), Rev. Walter Kelly (retired), Chaplains Coordinator for Toronto Police service (TPS), and Chaplain Brian Krushel with Camrose Police service (CPS)—for your encouragement and friendship. You are progressive and creative leaders!

- My two first and best police friends/brothers in Canada: retired Sergeant M. Bruce Fraser (Ontario Provincial Police) and the late Staff Sergeant Charles (Chuck) Lawrence (Royal Canadian Mounted Police). You opened my eyes to see and understand that in Canada, police officers are "real people" I can relate to as best friends. Thank you, sirs.

- Retired Staff Sergeant Al (Beulah) Marshall (RCMP), you are such an encouraging and caring leader with admirable people skills.

- Sergeant Craig Taylor (OPP), my soccer buddy in the Ottawa Valley. Your friendship on and off the soccer field was a great encouragement to me.

- Inspector Isobel Granger (Ottawa Police service), you blazed a trail

- My teachers/lecturers, especially th[...] impact on my life while I was on [...] Ocean, I cannot thank you enough[...] Manyengawana, Miss. D. Munemo, M[...] Fannuel Chandomba, Mr. Stewart [...] Dr. Robert Primrose, Mr. Robert O[...] You helped to lay a solid foundatio[...] educational journey.

- My friend, Monika B. Jensen, I met [...] Federation training in Toronto. You [...] encouragement to me: "Get the boo[...]

- Derrick Sweet, President of Certifie[...] for inspiring me to crystalize my dis[...] me to creatively find ways to put m[...] impact of my life experiences with [...] to Rod Macdonald (CEO of CCF) f[...] You were a great source of encourag[...]

- My faithful friends who have help[...] citizen: the late Wendell and Nora T[...] parents' in Canada. You were inspirati[...] Ruramai Mpindu - thank you for bein[...] Dr. Witness Jani (Auntie Mary and the[...] emotional and intellectual support. [...] Charles (Darla) Sutherland, for your l[...] life's uncertainties; Rajiv Dutt, for ins[...] box and envision my future; Catheri[...] determination and commitment to ex[...] Andriend (the late Roy) Schlievert, f[...] standing up against expressions of rac[...] for your unwavering love and support [...] (Colleen Schlievert), for your insigh[...] unwavering support and encouragem[...] for your friendship and support in va[...] friend; Lazarus Sidambe, for being a g[...] your friendship and encouragement; B[...] Normandeau, Carrie (Todd) Sparling,[...] Fraser, Arly Smith, the late Lila Fra[...]

into policing for visible minorities (now majorities), becoming the first black woman to rise to the rank of Inspector. You are a true "Zimbo" in the high ranks, my sister.

- Constable Aggrey Koech (Toronto Police service), for being a true *rafiki* (friend) indeed. You have been a great source of encouragement over the years.

- (Retired) Staff Sergeant Ezra (Tony) Browne, one of the first Black officers with YRP, who endured unimaginable and heart-wrenching conflicts (within and outside the organization) in those early years when it was rare to be a black police officer, when everyone else around you in the police family was white. You did not see that as a deterrent, but as an opportunity. Thank you for staying on course as a true conflict resolution practitioner. Your early experiences in policing deserve a separate book.

- Constable Laura Cullen, for showing up to diffuse a seemingly life-threatening situation that infused tremendous trust in the value of calling 9-1-1. You exemplified excellent alternative dispute and conflict resolution skills and professionalism.

- The late Constable Jason Ng, who died after a short bout with cancer. I observed you in action during my earliest rides-along as a chaplain. I was impressed by how you handled one potentially explosive conflict with friendliness, humour, calmness, tact, admirable professionalism, and mediation skills.

- The late Constable Garrett Styles, killed in the line of duty on Saturday, June 28, 2011, while attempting to resolve a conflict. You are my hero in life and in death. Even in your final words over the radio system, you encapsulated the sum of policing: determination, professionalism, and genuine care for the people you served. Indeed, life is so daily. I still recall shaking your hand and saying "congratulations" on your graduation from police training. You have a special place in my heart, just as you do in many hearts across York Region and beyond.

- My other special YRP friends, our giants, also killed in the line of duty while seeking to resolve conflicts: Detectives Rob Plunket (August 2007) and Doug Tribbling (August 1984); and PC William

Grant (October 1984). You const‌
conflicts are costly. Today, we se‌
are standing on your shoulders. T‌

- My Uganda Police friends: Supe‌
  Commander, Kampala Metropo‌
  Commandant at Police Training S‌
  the Zonal Commander, Kampal‌
  such a transformational leader wi‌
  Ssebo/sir. You gave me an oppo‌
  showcase some of the material an‌
  and conduct specialized worksh‌
  delivery in policing. The feedbac‌
  was inspiring. Superintendent Wi‌
  Department HQ in Kampala yo‌
  teachable spirit. I felt very safe t‌
  region of Uganda knowing that a‌
  was with us. Thank you, Ssebo/sir.

- My Jamaica Constabulary Police‌
  Division, Superintendent Dwight‌
  Winston Milton, and Detective C‌
  opportunity to participate in yo‌
  "quality customer service" to the‌
  You are innovative leaders.

- My Zimbabwe Republic Police‌
  Mazula, Assistant Inspector D‌
  (Masvingo)—for your efforts to‌
  engagement techniques and prac‌
  Township community (Zaka) des‌
  relationship with ZRP.

Community Related (friend‌

- Dr. Ken Penner, Professor of Ph‌
  College, you helped me to valu‌
  education in Africa. You stretched‌
  be reflective in my approach to lea‌

His formal academic journey began at Maungwe Primary School in Rusape, Zimbabwe, a small rural school he attended while living with his maternal grandmother (*Gogo Mudadi*). He completed his secondary education at St. Peter's Kubatana High & Technical School in Harare, Zimbabwe. Dr. (Munangi) Mpindu went on to complete several college and university degrees and diplomas:

- Evangelical Bible College, now Harare Theological College (Zimbabwe) – *Diploma in Religious Studies*

- Daystar University College (Kenya) – *Diploma in Communication Arts*

- Prairie College (Canada) – *Bachelor of Religious Education*

- Trinity Western University (Canada) – *Master of Theological Studies & Master of Divinity*

- University of Ottawa / St. Paul University (Canada) – *Master of Arts in Missions (Multiculturalism & Aboriginal Studies)*

- University of Pretoria (South Africa) – *PhD in Philosophy (Systematic Theology & Ethics)*

- York University (Canada) – *Postgraduate Certificate in Alternative Dispute and Conflict Resolution*

He also attended the Workplace Fairness Institute (Canada) to receive a *Certified Workplace Fairness Analyst (WFA designation),* and the Certified Coaches Federation (Canada) to be a *Certified Life Coach*. He has also taken specialized courses and training in other disciplines including leadership development, crisis management, emotional and mental wellness, and counselling.

Dr. (Munangi) Mpindu has been honoured to serve as a visiting lecturer in The Philippines, Jamaica, South Africa, India, Uganda, and Zimbabwe. Canada's indigenous people have a special place in his heart - and he has developed close friendships with some First Nations individuals and communities. He enjoys interacting with police officers in different jurisdictions around the world and learning about the uniqueness of the various communities in which they serve. In his spare time, he enjoys reading, driving, sightseeing, watching wildlife, watching and playing soccer (football), watching ice hockey and basketball, and listening to "new" country music. He thinks there are two types of music in the world: country and western. Given his appreciation for cultural diversity and inclusivity, he enjoys learning about different cultures, languages, and trying out different foods. He says, "Eating is natural, what you eat is cultural."

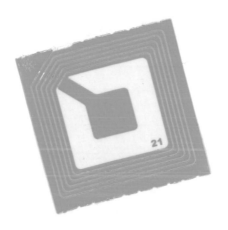